The Changing Face of Ross on Wye

The Changing Face of Ross on Wye

by
Tim Ward

Logaston Press

LOGASTON PRESS
Little Logaston Woonton Almeley
Herefordshire HR3 6QH
logastonpress.co.uk

First published by Logaston Press 2005
Copyright © Tim Ward 2005

ISBN 1 904396 42 9

Set in Times New Roman by Logaston Press
and printed in Great Britain by
Cromwell Press Ltd., Trowbridge

While writing this book I have come to appreciate more than ever all the known and unknown photographers of the last two centuries who have provided us with such a wealth of photographs for illustrating local history books. Their brilliant photographs of long forgotten scenes and events brighten the written word and bring their distant world into ours.

As a tribute I have appended a list of the early Ross photographers.

Contents

Acknowledgements

My sincere thanks are due to all the staff at the *Ross Gazette* office for their help and hospitality and also to the Record Office staff in Hereford for all their assistance in my researches for this book and other projects. Neither could I have managed without the local knowledge, anecdotes, patience and gifts of the people of Ross on Wye, Linden Alcock for his specialist knowledge of motor cars, all the authors of the books on Herefordshire that I have read in the 25 years I have lived in the county, and Ron Shoesmith for editing a mass of information into book form. I must also include my teachers at Colchester Royal Grammar School – Arthur Brown and 'Hiram' Hall – for first awakening my interest in history, and my wife, Shirley, for her support and unfailing patience.

By the same author

Herefordshire on old Postcards, Volume One
Herefordshire on old Postcards, Volume Two
Around Newent
Ledbury
Images of Childhood (with Colin Ward)
Herefordshire's Postcard Past

Introduction

One of the unexpected difficulties I encountered early on in my researches, was that references varied slightly in the information they gave. Recently a town councillor told me the reports of a meeting in two local papers varied not only from each other but also from what really happened. Three different versions of the same event only a week before! Reference books often gave differing information — is St. Mary's church spire 208 feet or 220 feet high? Were Rudhall's almshouses intended to be inhabited by men and women or just by single women? It becomes a matter of chance if a writer picks up the correct information or not. I have tried to get my facts right and to correct one or two previously published mistakes, but apologise if I have failed. There are occasional awkward discrepancies between Council records and press reports, usually concerning dates and finances. Difficulties also arise as early trade directories do not give street numbers.

The life of a town is constantly changing in response to the economic and social climate. The dynamics of life are development and change, sometimes faster, sometimes slower, but the last hundred years have certainly seen more rapid change in Ross than at any other time in its history. The simple street plan of feudal times based around the Church, the Market House and the Town Mill remains, but the town grows and buildings and businesses come, alter and disappear constantly. The slight traces that remain are often changed out of all recognition — the mill-pond in use for over a thousand years is now a car park; the railway's life was little more than a hundred years and leaves but a few buildings and bridges. Kemp's timber-yard began in Henry Street, moved to Millpond Street, was taken over and moved again to an industrial estate on Alton Lane. The military training camp for thousands of soldiers now provides employment in the factories built there. Even pubs close or change their names. The list goes on and on with cinemas, churches, factories and houses being built and used and reused or rebuilt as the times require. Even the town has changed its name! On 18 May 1931 Ross Urban District Council announced that Herefordshire County Council had authorised the change in name from Ross to Ross on Wye.

Tim Ward, September 2005

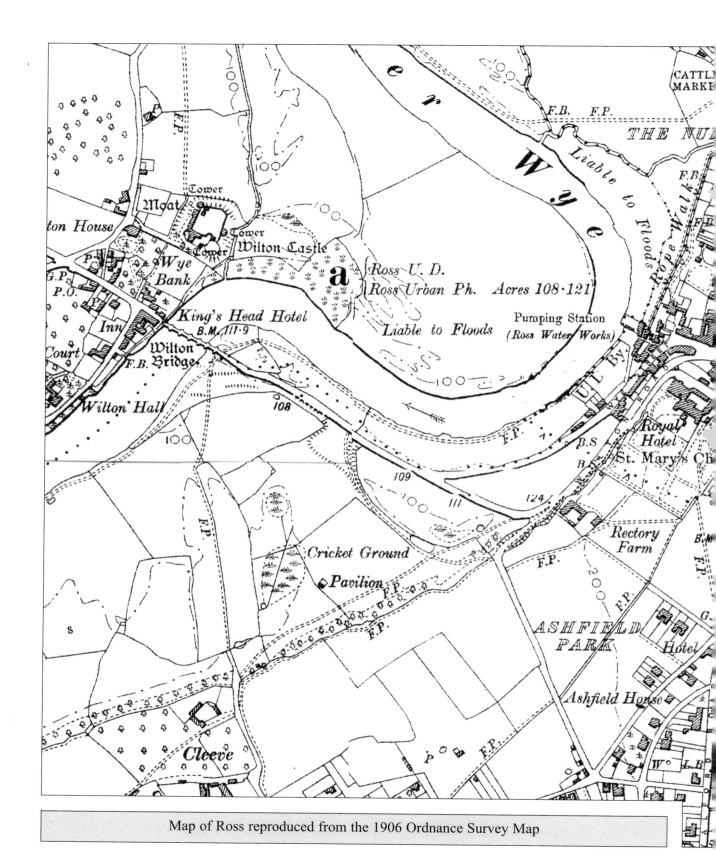

Map of Ross reproduced from the 1906 Ordnance Survey Map

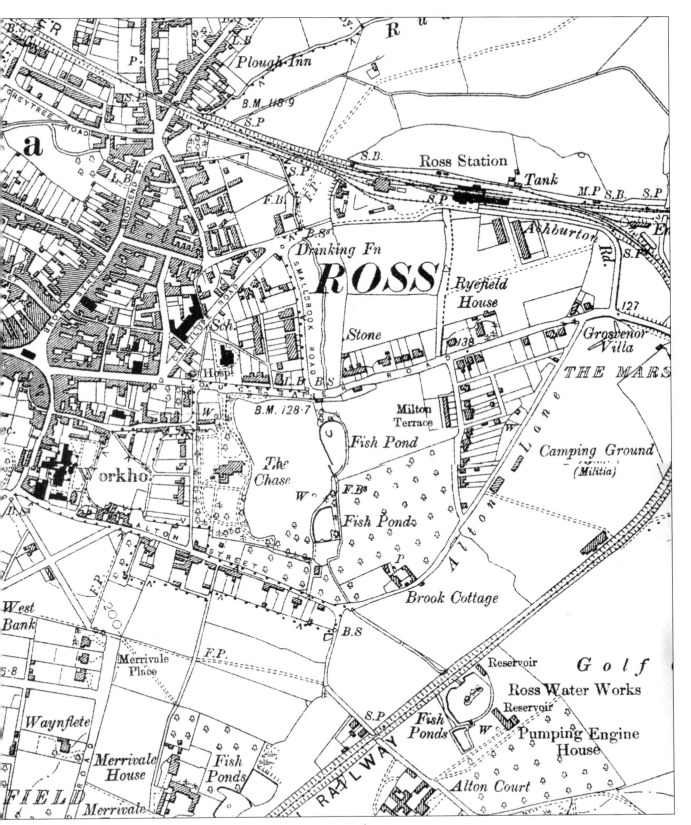

CHAPTER ONE

Ross — The Town and its Buildings

Ninety per cent of Herefordshire is composed of Old Red Sandstone providing a rich fertile soil for trees and crops. The small market town of Ross on Wye developed around a slight hill of this rock overlooking the river Wye on the junction of the roads to Ledbury, Hereford, Gloucester and Wales. Indeed, the name Ross derives from the Welsh or Celtic *rhos* meaning a hill or promontory referring to the higher ground around the church overlooking the horseshoe bend in the Wye 100 feet below. The fertile soil between the river valley and the hills must have given rich pickings to the hunter-gatherers of the Stone Age, and successive generations slowly cleared small fields from the woods that covered the whole area. About 2,500 years ago people built the massive ramparts surrounding the 19-acre hillfort on Chase Hill, where about 1,400 people lived for a time. This group controlled the district until the arrival of the Romans, who exploited the local iron ore. Although the Romans occupied the area for four hundred years they left no traces in the town of Ross, apart from a hoard of coins at Greytree. Their nearest settlement of any size was at Weston under Penyard a couple of miles from Ross.

Despite its proximity to the Welsh border, there was neither a castle nor any defensive earthworks, although the nearest castle was close by at Wilton. This was built in the early Norman period to guard the ford just down-stream from the present bridge, itself built in 1599.

At an unknown date burgage plots (building plots), for the tradesmen and shopkeepers who had established themselves along the main streets, were formally set out. Their lines are still recognisable in the long, narrow shop premises and especially from maps and aerial photographs. Whilst most were probably of Norman origin, these burgage plots could date back to Anglo-Saxon times, around 900, when King Ethelred of Mercia was building new, fortified towns like Oxford and Shrewsbury or rebuilding old ones like Worcester and Gloucester and setting out similar plots for their inhabitants.

The entry for Ross in the *Domesday Book* reveals how extensively agriculture had developed around the town during the Anglo-Saxon period.

> In Ross 7 hides which pay tax. In lordship 1 plough; another would be possible. 18 villagers and 6 smallholders and a priest with 23 ploughs. 3 slaves, a mill at 6s. 8d., meadow, 16 acres. The wood-land is in the King's Enclosure. The villagers pay 18s. in dues.

(A 'hide' was a measure of land equating to about 120 acres, whilst a 'plough' also included the oxen to pull it.) In 1086 the Bishop of Hereford was lord of the manor, owning most of the surrounding land; hence the 23 ploughs. The mill mentioned was that at Brookend, which harnessed the power of the Rudhall Brook, and a small nucleus of houses developed around it. It can also be assumed that a church was erected in a dominant position on the site of St. Mary's overlooking the growing cluster of houses between it and the corn mill. People came to the market place to barter and trade long before the official establishment of a market there in 1138 — really only another way to tax the inhabitants and raise income for the church authorities.

Despite incursions by the Welsh, famine, plagues and civil wars, Ross managed to grow slowly over the centuries as it absorbed people displaced by disaster, economic upheavals and later land enclosures or those lured by the thought of settled work in a developing market town. The 16th century saw the first mention

ROSS-ON-WYE FROM THE AIR.

On 18 May 1931 Ross Urban District Council announced that Herefordshire County Council had authorised the change in name from Ross to Ross on Wye, so this superb aerial view from the east was published after that date. The original layout of the town in medieval times is shown by the narrow houses and the strips of garden or cluster of buildings in the rear. The Market House and St. Mary's church with the Wye beyond stand out clearly. Note the lack of development in Old Maid's Walk and the top of Church Street on the left of the photo and the size of the Ross Union Workhouse in the foreground, now rebuilt as Ross Community Hospital. The large building to the right was Bellamy's foundry, demolished in the 1920s and now, after a chequered history, redeveloped as the attractive Crofts shopping precinct.

Airco was one of several aerial photographic firms based at Hendon airfield outside London in the 1920s. Started by young pilots who had been trained for action in the First World War, these firms had chequered fortunes and were mostly short-lived, but they left an important legacy of aerial photographs of most of the towns and villages in the country, revealing much detail to present-day historians. Broad Street and Edde Cross Street are prominent in the evening sunshine.

A detailed look at this fine, anonymous photograph of Ross taken from the church tower about 1910 shows some of the changes that have taken place in and around the town in the last hundred years. The nearby roofscape has changed little, but the original Methodist Church in Edde Cross Street, nearly opposite Merton House, has been replaced by a modern building. The gas works chimney in the centre has long gone, together with the rows of cottages in Morley Square now replaced by smart modern houses. Beyond the cattle market and the railway embankment there were allotments, carefully cultivated for their fresh vegetables in an age when every penny had to stretch as far as possible. Houses now replace the cattle market at the bottom of Edde Cross Street and cover half the land at Springfield Farm and Cawdor at the top left. Most of the rows of cottages at the Nursery have also been replaced by modern housing and bright flower beds. 1930s and '50s Council housing covers the land in the top right corner where most of the houses up Brampton Road were demolished in the slum clearances of the 1930s.

The well kept gardens of the old rectory in this 1930 aerial photograph disappeared in the following 30 years. In 1935 a new rectory was built on the kitchen garden in the corner of Church Street and Old Maid's Walk replacing the uneconomic Georgian building which was temporarily used as a police station until a new one was built in 1957 costing £25,413. A large house, until 2000 a doctor's surgery, stands between the two. The old rectory was demolished in 1957 giving access to the new police houses in Church Close, built to replace substandard housing elsewhere.

Above: The sight of these happy children outside the Congregational church in Gloucester Road in the summer of 1908 provided a stunning photograph by Colman Debenham. This was the Ross United Reformed Church Sunday School outing to Walford Court. The children cheerfully crowd into the first wagon looking forward to games before the bunfight provided by the fashionable ladies in the smaller farm wagon. The third wagon, carrying the food and drink, was operated by R.T. Smith and Co. for the Great Western Railway, on loan for the occasion. H.O. Wills, the Bristol cigarette manufacturer, laid the foundation stone of the church on 3 June 1867. The building cost £1,900 with seating for 420 people. The church is still externally the same although it now houses an attractive antiques centre.

Left: The Wesleyan chapel in Edde Cross Street, with a schoolroom at the back, was erected in 1867 at a cost of £1,175 during a decade of nonconformist church building in Ross. This photograph dates from about 1905. The old chapel saw about a century of use until it was replaced by a building more suitable to modern needs in 1972.

of glove, hat, shoe, nail and basket making in Ross, together with leather work (harness making). These industries recur in the records of each century until the early 20th.

The 18th century saw an increasing amount of small scale industry in Ross. By 1747 Land Tax returns show a tannery, nailmakers, metalworks, leather works, a shoe factory, a mill and a brewery in the Brookend area. The Pritchard family living at Brookend House owned the tannery upon which the leather and shoe industries were at least partly dependent. The Town Mill and warehouses were rebuilt about this period on a site which had made use of the power of the Rudhall Brook for nearly a thousand years. The gradual development of industries from this nucleus in Brookend led to a rash of cheap houses being built for their workers; by 1817 houses extended up Overross and by 1830 had reached Brookfield Road off Brampton Street. This ever-increasing pressure of house building, new roads and industries in the 19th and 20th centuries removed the smallholdings, orchards and little fields that previously mingled with the townscape of Ross.

As the country recovered from the economic depression after the Napoleonic wars, Ross started to prosper. Country towns were very self-sufficient and Ross was no exception, with a galaxy of shops to supply local needs. In 1835 the following industries were recorded: a brewer, four coopers, three curriers, three tanners, five saddle and harness makers, a glover, eight maltsters, five corn millers, five wheelwrights, three braziers, three basketmakers, 14 boot and shoemakers, three cabinetmakers, eight dressmakers, 17 builders, two woolstaplers, two whitesmiths, three nailmakers, four watch and clock makers, two pumpmakers, a fellmonger, two clogmakers, two staymakers, five straw hat makers, a ropemaker, a boat builder, four soap and tallow boilers, and a timber merchant. There were four banks to finance these enterprises, whilst eight coaches ran daily to other parts of the kingdom and 11 long distance carriers transported finished articles to distant markets. There were also innumerable local carriers serving the local villages. For some reason blacksmiths are not mentioned, but it can be presumed there were several to shoe the horses on which all this road transport depended. The river was too prone to varying water levels, shifting shoals and rapids to become a reliable route for barge traffic, which in any event ceased with the construction of the Hereford to Gloucester canal and the arrival of the railway in 1855. However, the advent of tourists and associated boat hire to explore the Wye valley added to the number of men employed on the river from 1745 until 1914 when pleasure boating dwindled, never to recover its former popularity. Landing places have all but disappeared and trees have grown along the river banks since the towpaths were abandoned.

The Ross to Monmouth railway was opened in 1873. Railway companies provided large scale employment at a time when every possible care was taken to give service to their passengers and customers. As the century progressed other industries developed in Ross. The gas works in Kyrle Street provided both employment and houses for their workers in Morley Square and Kyrle Street. The Kell brothers developed an agricultural machinery works by the mill pond, and Kemp's timber yard in Henry Street opened. To keep order in this bustling town there were 11 constables, two sergeants and a superintendent based in the Police Station in Brampton Street beside the railway viaduct.

Thus, as the 19th century progressed, a thriving town centre much as we know it today can be imagined. Ribbon development of poor-quality houses existed along Overross and Brampton Streets and Old Gloucester Road. The area between Edde Cross and Broad Streets, Millpond Street and the Nursery were full of small houses for the workers in Ross's growing industries. Some of these people had been displaced from the surrounding countryside by the Enclosure Acts which were designed in part to provide a pool of cheap labour for farmers and businessmen and remove people's spirit of independence for ever. To pick up the casualties of this process, 1837 saw the building of the Ross Union Workhouse under the 1834 Poor Law legislation.

One interesting development of the thriving Ross of the 1860s was the rapid construction of nonconformist churches. A new Wesleyan chapel was built in Edde Cross Street in 1866. The next year the

Plymouth Brethren church in Henry Street opened. A Congregational church in Gloucester Road replaced an earlier one in Kyrle Street in 1868. A Mission Room was built in Overross in 1880 and the following year the Baptist church in Broad Street, founded in 1819, was rebuilt. Depending on the strength of their congregations some of these have survived the years while others have succumbed to the harsh economics of the 20th century and have found other uses more suitable to the times.

The Victorian era saw more and better houses being built for the well-off away from the poorer areas. An advertisement in the *Ross Gazette* on 16 March 1871 read:

> Allotment of Freehold land. The Ross and Archenfield Benefit Building Society having purchased an estate at Springfield, the same has been staked out for allotments into 54 shares, which will be balloted on Tuesday next. Members who are one week in arrears will not be eligible.

These allotments were in fact building plots, costing their fortunate owners £33 each and are now known as Greytree. (The new residents had to wait a hundred years before their unmade road, in some places just bare slippery rock, was properly surfaced in the early 1970s.) Cheap imports of grain from America and beef from Argentina caused a severe agricultural depression that lasted until 1914, and as a result from 1871 onwards the owners of Springfield farm started selling off building land until by the end of the 20th century the whole farm was covered in houses.

One of Ross's most notable Victorian businessmen, and benefactors, was Thomas Blake. Blake was born above his parents' hardware shop on the corner of Station Street and Brookend Street. From early on he was an entrepreneur and was twice M.P. for Leominster. He eventually owned an ironworks and foundry in Broad Street, Ross, the latter employing enough men to field its own football team. He was particularly concerned at the lack of a clean water supply to the town — in the 1880s half the houses in Ross had no water supply and depended on three public pumps or a dubious supply from the Wye. At that time there were 143 private shallow wells. To fulfill his dream of clean, pure water for every house in the town, Thomas Blake purchased the 175-acre Alton Court Estate from Ephraim Hallum for £11,000 in 1890, an acquisition that included the Territorial Army rifle range and the Ross Golf Club. Thanks to his previous parliamentary experience he was able to obtain an Act of Parliament, the Ross Water Act of 1892, enabling him to carry through his dream and incidentally giving him a money-spinning monopoly. The offices of the Water Company were at 44 Broad Street.

Most of the materials for this massive enterprise came from Blake's extensive hardware business. One of the Blake family's advertisements in 1906 stated they had supplied and installed Crossley oil engines ('the best available') to drive duplicate pumps for the town's water supply at Alton Court Works and for other industrial uses in and around Ross. The quality of their materials and workmanship is still evident in the remaining buildings, and the system, which cost £30,000, continued in use for many years and was eventually taken over by Welsh Water in 1974.

THOMAS BLAKE, Esq.

Opposite: With the skilled help of his nephew, Henry T. Blake, who owned the family business in Brookend Street, Thomas Blake sank three artesian boreholes into the sandstone and installed a pumping house and machinery to pump water up the hill to a covered reservoir from which five and a half miles of pipe distributed it throughout the town from Brampton Abbots to Tudorville. The huge, environmentally friendly windpump, 35 feet in diameter was installed as part of the pumping system (compare the height of the men on the platform).

Left: 'Our shop' says the message on this postcard of their shop in Station Street, and what a shop it was in 1907! Blakes sold everything imaginable from kettles to farmers' multi-bay Dutch barns for hay and straw. Their hydraulic machinery was installed at Alton Court Waterworks, housed in buildings of their own design and manufacture, delivering water through Blakes' taps and boiled in Blakes' kettles. Trade has come full circle and in 2003 the old shop became a hardware store once again.

No. 622.

The Original Accounts should be presented at the time of payment.

Ross Water Undertaking.

WATER WORKS OFFICE,
GLOUCESTER ROAD,
ROSS-ON-WYE.

14 DEC. 1933

Mr. Pascoe..

Denstone, WestonGrove, Ross.

Dear Sir (or Madam),

We beg to remind you that you have not yet paid your Water Rate for the current half-year, due ....29 SEP. 1933..... last.

We therefore request that **at an early date** we are favoured with a remittance to this office for the amount due.

Yours faithfully,

ROSS WATER UNDERTAKING.

Amount Due, £ 2 : 15 : 4d.

Gazette, Printers, Ross.

A gentle reminder of an unpaid bill for £2 15s. 4d.

Thomas Blake also put much effort and over £3,000 into rebuilding the Baptist church in Broad Street, including a memorial pulpit to his first wife. As a memorial after his own death in 1901, the town spent £660 and cleared a rough sloping piece of ground, where some cottages had once stood, leading down to the Hope and Anchor Inn. They then installed steps, seats, plants and trees, naming the area the Blake Memorial Gardens. His old firm became a public company in 1910.

Modern local government was initiated by the 1835 Municipal Reform Act and under the subsequent Ross Improvement Act, the town was run by 12 Town Commissioners. Although styled a borough there was no corporation, as existed in larger towns, nor did it exercise municipal functions. A court leet was held at Michaelmas (29 September) at which the town officers were appointed and a jury of the court leet chose a mayor.

This was put on a more businesslike basis by the 1894 Local Government Act when Ross was divided into Ross Urban of 436 acres and 4,305 inhabitants (including the nine officials and 96 inmates of the Union Workhouse), whilst Ross Rural's area was 2,682 acres with a population of just 620. Ross Urban District Council took over its administrative functions in April 1896 with responsibility for the town's roads, public health, markets, fire brigade, and an infectious diseases hospital. It had power to raise

Appropriately, this postcard was addressed to Frederick Cooper, Rosedale, Ashfield with the short message, 'Blake Memorial. Subcommittee to meet Col. Middleton 11 am at the Dock'. Col. Middleton was chairman of the Ross Urban District Council and they were meeting to inspect the finished work at the gardens in September 1908. Thomas Blake, the youngest boy in a family of six, rose by his own talents to be a J.P. and an M.P. with a variety of business interests and should rank high above John Kyrle as a long-term benefactor to his home town. Among his achievements he rebuilt the Baptist Church, installed a clean water supply for the town, secured a permanent future for the Prospect, and gave the old Town Council offices in Broad Street which included a library. He also preached widely in the area and was a member of many committees running the town, including the Ross Board of Guardians that was responsible for the workhouse. That this memorial garden should be enjoyed by everybody in Ross would surely have been his wish.

rates and could borrow money. The 1875 Public Health Act, the 1870 and 1902 Education Acts and the Housing Act of 1909 laid the foundations for the vast improvements in health, education and housing that are still enjoyed today. These powers were progressively increased during the 20th century as the need arose to clear slums and build social housing.

Most of these powers were removed to South Herefordshire District Council in the 1974 local government reorganisation (and subsequently to the present Herefordshire Council). The County Council had been established by the 1888 Local Government Act with initial responsibilities for roads between towns, bridges, poor relief and mental health asylums. In local government terms the 1974 reorganization reduced Ross on Wye Town Council to parish council status although, paradoxically, it could elect a mayor again.

From as early as 1086, and possibly even before that date, a mill has stood on the site of Town Mill. Rebuilt several times over the years the present buildings date from the 18th century. Various industries developed in this area and workers' houses were built along the surrounding roads. In the late 17th century the mill owner built an imposing town residence overlooking the mill pond. In 1851 the house was converted into the Railway Inn (later called the Railway Hotel for a time).

For centuries the mill pond provided the motive power for the mill machinery, but the flow of the Rudhall Brook was not always sufficient to run the mill full time. In 1895 Bussell & Pike installed steam boilers to improve the efficiency and reliability needed; note the chimney behind the earlier buildings. This idyllic postcard masks the reality of the prevailing conditions at the old mill pond in Edwardian times. After centuries of continual use it fell into disuse and decay and became silted up as it was not regularly flushed out by the force of water driving the mill-wheel. An added factor was sewage running into it from nearby cottages in Overross and from a urinal. By 1900 residents were complaining of the smell and the Sanitary Inspector was asked to devise a means to alleviate the nuisance. By the terms of a seven-year lease, the Council took over the mill pond for a rent of 1s. annually from 1 January 1902. They agreed to remove the urinal, to fill in the pond without impeding the flow of the stream, sow grass seed and 'dedicate the site and maintain same during such term as an Ornamental Garden [so as] to avoid obnoxious effussions in Summer'. This came to be called King's Acre in commemoration of King Edward VII's birthday. The flower beds are just visible on the far side of the pond below the railway embankment in the top photo. The disused sluice controlling water levels is visible on the left and the shallowness of the water can be judged by the way the ducks are preening.

After continuing complaints about smells and flies, in 1925–26 the Sanitary Inspector, Frank Ricketts, reported the mill pond as 'a distinct danger to the health of the town', partly because Ross Engineering and South Herefordshire Agricultural Co-operative Society's stables and drains emptied into it. One councillor, who appreciated the loss of the proposed children's play area in Millpond Street, suggested the millpond be drained and surfaced to provide 'a play area for the poor children of Brampton Street, who can only play in the streets', but he got no support. The whole pond was finally filled with rubble in 1927 after further complaints about smells and flies, whereupon the Co-operative Society successfully sued the council for £48 15s. 2d. for undertaking the work. In the 1950s the Society used the area for a time to display chicken huts of various types. Other people remember it as rough waste grassland. In 1961, after the opening of the M50, plans were suggested to turn the site into a 'bus and coach station. Nothing came of this idea and eventually the present Five Ways car park was constructed on the site.

Over the years a succession of millers ran the Town Mill. By 1895 the Partnership of Bussell and Pike started modernising it with steam power and by 1906 they were using a steam lorry for deliveries.

On 24 April 1919 the Ross Branch of the National Farmers Union suggested the idea of a farmers' co-operative. Rapid negotiations resulted in the registration of the South Herefordshire Agricultural Co-operative Society (SHACS) on 26 August 1919, with a head office at their shop 3/4 Gloucester Road. The temporary president was H.J. Pike and the secretary J.H. Marfell. On 29 November Russell and Pike's corn milling and seed firm was transferred to SHACS for £7,400. Charles Russell became their traveller and SHACS was in business. 1920 showed a profit of £3,750 and they were able to open a branch in Coleford in November. More expansion followed with the amalgamation of Monmouth Agricultural Co-operative Society on 1 January 1924. The growing agricultural depression, the 1926 coal strike and a serious fire in 1930, costing their insurers £2,882, all contributed in keeping their profits down until conditions improved in 1935. Plans were drawn up for a warehouse on the old mill pond and to expand along Brookend Street, but they came to nothing. Wartime years saw a boom in profits which continued to rise steadily until in the 1970s SHACS became part of the Countrywide Group and moved to Ledbury.

In 1973 there was a proposal to demolish the Railway Hotel as part of a road widening scheme. Fortunately its sound construction and historic architectural value saved it from demolition. The whole area is a reminder of the wealth earned by the industries in this part of the town. This in turn generated the sturdy nonconformity and free thinking shown in the long-established Friends' Meeting House nearby.

The shop next to the Railway Inn, as it became, was occupied by a number of different businesses over the years and now, together with the Town Mill, is part of Easter and Steele's furniture showrooms. In the 1920s and '30s it was the Ross Drug Stores, owned by Nicholl & Co., being conveniently placed for the large number of people then living in that part of town. 'National Insurance Dispensing' says the sign in the window.

OLD ALMSHOUSES ROSS

PRINCE of WALES

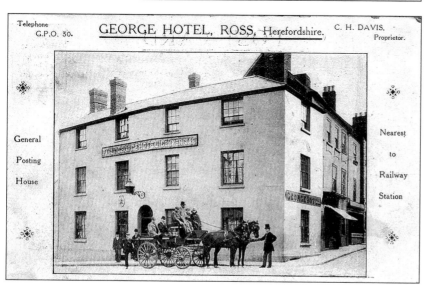

GEORGE HOTEL, ROSS, Herefordshire.

C. H. DAVIS,
Proprietor.

General

Posting

House

Nearest

to

Railway

Station

Top: Rudhall's Almshouses in Church Street were intended for five poor men or women (or possibly just women) who were each given an allowance of 30s. *per annum.* These five tiny almshouses were altered in 1960 to accommodate three elderly people, though externally they remain unchanged. The adjoining double-doored shed was also converted into a smart town house in keeping with its neighbours. Since Richard Worcester built four almshouses in Old Gloucester Road in 1510 to house four elderly destitute inhabitants (these were named after Perrock who endowed them in 1605), other wealthy benefactors established similar almshouses which did much to alleviate the suffering of the poor and old. They continued in use until the 20th century and saved many the shame of entering the workhouse to end their days.

Middle: The ever popular Prince of Wales Inn on the way out to Walford looks much the same from the outside although the trees and the garden have inevitably seen some 90 years of change since this 1916 photograph. The main entrance has been moved to the rear of the building facing the car park while the interior has been largely amalgamated into one large open space.

Bottom: A rare advertising postcard of the George Hotel which stood on the corner of Gloucester Road and Copse Cross Street until demolished in 1960. The hotel's horse-drawn brake stands outside in the quiet street ready to take guests on a sightseeing tour. On 20 July 1912 C.H. Davis, the proprietor, used this card to send Mr. Williams, a farmer at Ryeford, the message: 'Dear Mr. W. Flying exhibitions tomorrow at 11 am & 4 pm. Yours C.H. Davis'. Delivery was virtually guaranteed!

Left: A chauffeur awaits patiently as his master, in holiday attire of straw boater and plimsolls, vies for the photographer's attention as a horse rider takes precedence in the picture. This is a lovely snapshot of Edwardian life outside the King's Head Hotel in the High Street. It was taken about 1909 when the motor car was making its first tentative appearance on the streets of Ross.

Note the window boxes full of flowers long before 'Britain in Bloom' competitions, and the ornate lamp brackets over the hotel doorway. Behind the plain 19th-century façade lie concealed the fine timbers of the original coaching hotel.

Below: The King's Head was advertising a complete renovation in 1867 together with the addition of the Swan yard and stabling for 100 horses. These alterations were designed as much to attract tourists as to accommodate the needs of local farmers visiting the stock market at the top of nearby Wye Street and Edde Cross Street.

SWAN HOTEL, ROSS, HEREFORDSHIRE, The nearest Hotel to the River Wye.
BILLIARDS. Posting in all its Branches. Telephone, No. 44 P.O. Address, Manageress.

Top and middle: In 1876 the Swan Hotel Company advertised shares to raise £6,000 capital to build a new hotel aimed at the growing numbers of tourists in Ross and also to cater for the large numbers of farmers and buyers who thronged the streets outside the hotel on market days. The foundation stone was laid in April that year, but changes of fortune have involved modifications in the years since then. This pair of photographs show progressive changes during a 30-year period. More recently, the corner doorway has been reinstated as an entrance to the Tourist Information Centre. The horse-drawn omnibus met every train at the station in case there were guests for the hotel. For a time William Pulling & Co., a Hereford firm, ran a wine and spirit store on the corner at No. 1 High Street. By the end of the 1930s the Swan had become part of the Trust Houses group, and Pulling's old shop became the public bar with a new entrance just along the street. A board outside the main entrance advertises coach tours, while RAC signboards point to Ledbury and Gloucester.

Bottom: Internal photographs are by no means common as early film and photographic plates were not sensitive enough to cope with low light levels. Flash photography was only possible by igniting a magnesium flare which could be dangerous. Altogether, this is an unusual view of the dining room in the Crown and Sceptre. Mrs. Blake was obviously proud of the flower-decorated dining table she had laid on for the Royal Antidiluvian Order of Buffaloes (R.A.O.B.) on the night of 7 March 1907. This was a working men's association to ensure financial support for members and their families in time of need.

Top: Despite the competition from the Swan Hotel opposite, the Valley Hotel continued in business for many years at the top of Edde Cross Street, claiming to be the nearest hotel to the river Wye. Its mock-Tudor timbered façade has now been removed and the building converted into separate houses.

Middle: This hotel passed into the Trust Houses group in the 1930s and boasted similar facilities to its rivals, but additionally provided a grass tennis court for the benefit of its guests. It was about this time, in 1934, that Ross Urban District Council spent £234 constructing hard tennis courts at Crossfield to entertain residents and to attract visitors.

Bottom: The photograph of the reception area in the Valley Hotel, with comfortable sofas and pictures of the Ross locality on the walls, was one of a series of publicity postcards made about 1920. The owner, Holmwood Caws, commissioned R.E. Davies to produce them in an endeavour to encourage more trade.

John Kyrle's old house became an inn after his death and was later divided into two premises. After a succession of owners the *Ross Gazette* took over part from 1915 until 2003. The half further from the camera was owned by a series of chemists: Cary, Cocks and Roper; Thomas Roper; J.H. Hart and J.F. Hart whose sign hangs over the door. These chemists sold everything to cure anything, at least according to the labels. The piquant flavour of Herefordshire Sauce once rivalled Worcester Sauce, but the recipe is now lost. In the 1920s, at the time of this photograph, 36 High Street (on the right) was owned by W. Raymond, a chiropodist, who attended only on Thursdays.

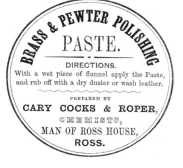

Top right: As the effects of the Industrial Revolution slowly penetrated into rural 19th-century Herefordshire, so new industries appeared in Ross providing much needed employment for the growing population.

Messrs. Kell Brothers started their iron foundry and agricultural machinery works in Millpond Street in 1847. Despite a lack of prosperity in farming generally they slowly expanded, and by 1901 they were advertising a wide range of ploughs, cultivators, rollers, corndrills etc. made in their works in Ross and Gloucester; they also had branches in Hereford and Leominster.

In addition the firm was agent for Bamlett's farm machinery from Thirsk in Yorkshire. Some of their machinery is depicted on this photograph probably taken at the Royal Agricultural Show in Gloucester in 1908. On 1 January 1913 Kells sold their manufacturing works to George Whitcher to concentrate on selling and repairing farm machinery from enlarged showroom premises opposite the old works.

Bottom right: Connie Dean stands beside her Christmas window display (about 1930). Packed full of toys, a teddy bear, dolls, crackers, gifts and decorations, it was a mouth-watering sight for two little boys.

Albert James Dean, her father, was listed in *Kelly's Directory* in 1926 and '37 as the owner of 30 and 31 Broad Street, but Connie ran the shop until at least 1970; it is now remembered as a general store and junk shop. She recently died at the age of 95. It is now home to Ross Electrics, opposite the end of Station Street.

17

The Market House has always been regarded as a meeting place for the people of Ross. Consequently, when the Bishop of Hereford conducted a tour of his diocese on 12 May 1923, Ross Urban District Council offered him the Market House as a venue for an open-air afternoon service. He certainly achieved his aim of taking the church to the people by preaching to the crowds assembled there. Some were hanging out of the windows if not onto his every word. The children, however, seemed more interested in the anonymous photographer than in their new, energetic bishop, the Right Reverend Martin Linton Smith.

Three charabancs and a variety of cars, neatly parked in front of the Market House in this 1925 photograph, must have brought about 100 visitors to the town. Even at that time parked coaches and charabancs were causing problems for the Council who gave the police a list of 24 sites for coaches to await their passengers in an attempt to keep the Market House clear for cars. Present parking requirements means that there are far fewer coach parties than in previous years and consequently less trade. What could be better for trade in Ross than if this area by the Market Hall was marked out with painted lines for coaches to unload their passengers in the very centre of the town? Note the little road on the right which was well used until closed to traffic in the late 1970s as a start to pedestrianisation.

Right: In medieval times Alton Street was the main route into Ross from the east. It became a quiet backwater when Old Gloucester Road and then Gloucester Road came into use. Walking up the centre of the road is a group of ladies carrying bundles (of wood?) on their heads, African style, while a couple of children pause with their barrowload of firewood to watch Dickie Davies at work. No longer a tranquil scene, in recent years it has been transformed by the increase in traffic displaced by the one-way system and squeezed into a road built for horse transport.

Market pens empty as the cattle are driven away and buyers and farmers turn their attention to the crowded sheep pens. A throng of farmers, stockmen and buyers surround Cooper & Preece's auctioneer in this busy 1910 scene. The stout fence of railway sleepers was intended to prevent animals straying onto the railway line. The cattle market was opened on 25 September 1871, replacing street markets in Edde Cross Street, New Street and at the Swan corner where conditions had become squalid. J.H. Skyrme, Clerk to the Town Commissioners offered this piece of land between the railway embankment and Greytree Road as a convenient new site. Apart from the obvious improvements to the town in cleanliness and lack of disruption, farmers and buyers benefited by quick access to the railway to dispatch their animals to the abbatoirs of South Wales and the Midlands. It served the area well for many years until moved to the bypass in 1988. In 1990 much of the embankment from where this photograph was taken was levelled to make way for new housing at New Market Close.

THE CENTRAL CAFÉ

Phone ROSS 2193

Opposite noted old Market House in the centre of the town

MORNING COFFEE
LUNCHEONS
TEAS

Private Rooms available for Parties

MENU ON REQUEST

Bakers & Confectioners

A Large Selection of Chocolates and Sweets by the Best British and Continental Makers in Stock

R.A.C. APPOINTED

MEMBER OF BRITISH HOTELS AND RESTAURANTS ASSOCIATION

A 1950s guidebook provides this view of the well-stocked interior of the Central Café. Its comfortable upstairs room, overlooking the Market Place, is still remembered fondly by the older generation for its relaxing atmosphere. Although renamed, it still retains its popularity with local people and visitors alike.

Above: This is an enlargement of a 1906 photograph taken from Chase Hill near the waterworks. A great amount of building has now filled the foreground with factories along Alton Lane and houses between there and the railway where the big water tank marks the eastern end of the station. The two rows of terrace houses in North Road were opposite the station entrance.

The large shed and tall chimney to the right belonged to the Ross Tannery. The two small fields beside the factory contained pits and vats for part of the tanning process. Tanning converts fresh animal skins and hides into workable leather by steeping them for varying amounts of time in vats filled with a solution of tannin derived from oak bark readily available in the locality. In 1867 there were two tanners in Ross — William Watkins in Broad Street, and George Smyth & Co who established the Ross Tannery in 1837 at the end of Tanyard Lane where the smell was well away from the town. There were four harness makers and 16 boot and shoe makers listed in Ross at this time, using the locally produced leather. Local craft industries like this were present in towns throughout the country until specialisation, mass production and easy transport either put them out of business, or changed them to retailers of goods made in other parts of the country.

The houses in the centre were an area known as the Folly, near the laundry on the Ledbury Read. The houses on the left had just been built in Camp Road. There is even Dickie Davies' thumbprint on the right where he handled the damp print before it was completely dry!

Right: The Royal Hotel omnibus meanders its quiet way up Cantilupe Road after collecting a visitor from the railway station. Modern redevelopment has altered this corner of Ross where Arthur Wheale ran the Wye Valley Cycle and Gun Works for many years. On the left of the photograph the Wallace Hall monument, a memorial to a 19th-century philanthropist, has been moved to accommodate the traffic roundabout needed to cope with the flow of vehicles outside Morrison's supermarket.

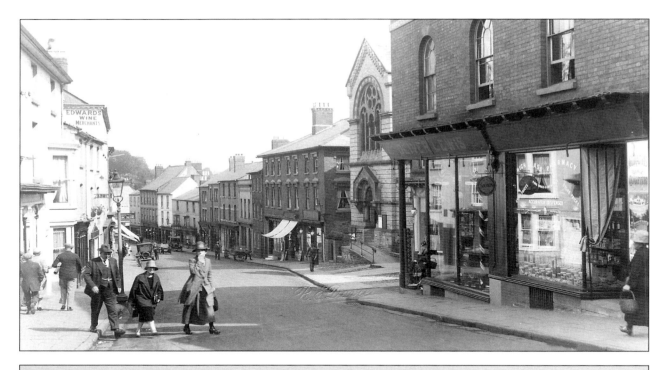

Above: Except for a change in ownership and merchandise these shop buildings have changed little since this 1920 photograph was taken by R.E. Davies. The passing years naturally see developments in all sorts of ways in the growth of the town, some slight and some dramatic. Benjamin's, the chemists, moved out of these premises in 2004. Oliver Lewis sold linen, fabrics and bedding at No. 50 next door on the corner of the Crofts. The entrance to the Baptist church, opened in 1870, has recently been rebuilt to make it more user friendly. The ladies in fashionable cloche hats would have more difficulty crossing the street now with all the congestion arising from the large numbers of cars using Broad Street. Edwards, the wine merchants, were prominent halfway down in what is now the Charles II Inn. Built in 1934 Woolworths now dominates the north side of the street, but the really noticeable difference is the increase in traffic.

Left: Gloucester Road outside the Chase Hotel in 1906 as a pony and trap heads off towards Weston under Penyard. The houses opposite were built during the 1880s in a period of economic growth. The grass verge beside the Chase wall remained for many years until 1937, when the Council found enough money to make it into a proper pavement as part of a road resurfacing scheme between the Chase Hotel gates and 'Lake View'.

Right: New Street in the summer of 1907, overlooked by Merton House. This street still retains much of its character although many of the poorer houses on the east (right-hand) side have been rebuilt.

The house on the left served as the Dispensary until the building of the Cottage Hospital.

Above: An Automobile Association patrolman and a policeman wearing white gloves for traffic duty confer on the state of traffic at the Cross one Autumn day c.1930 as townspeople go about their daily business around them. It is quite plain from this photograph by R.E. Davies how wide the road is and how much traffic it could accommodate before it was narrowed by planners and road engineers. Passey & Halls' garage was next door to the Post Office for many years. They made use of their prominent gable-end wall as an advertisement hoarding for BSA and Raleigh cycles and motor cycles. Note the George on the right and the gaps in the frontage beyond that were not filled with shops until the 1960s rebuilding scheme. Yet despite the apparent lack of motor traffic in the streets the *Ross Gazette* was reporting more and worse accidents than happen these days!

Above: The Kyrle Picture Palace, opposite the end of Cantilupe Road, was completed in 1913, virtually finishing the building along Gloucester Road begun a hundred years earlier. Small and Ashton, the architects, designed the building to seat 200 people on the ground floor and 50 in the balcony. It also had changing rooms for variety acts to entertain the audience between films. Early films were mostly short, so every week Edwin Dekin advertised different variety acts to perform between films. There were two performances at 6.30 and 8.30 pm and matinees on Thursdays and Saturdays. Seats cost 1s., 6d. and 3d. For the first year he provided free seats for inhabitants of the Union Workhouse. He also hoped to use the hall for other events when no films were available. By 1920 trade must have fallen seriously as Dekin filled every available space with so much old furniture from his antique business next door that the Sanitary Inspector was forced to issue him a warning to make exits and other areas safe for the Ross youngsters to enjoy the escapist pleasures of his cinema in safety. On the extreme left of the photograph, next door at No. 14, R.E. Davies had a photographic studio for many years at least until 1950, but it is evident from this postcard that for a time it housed Hill and Dickin's corn merchant's office. An advertisement for Thorley's cattle food can be seen in the window.

Below: Two 1867 advetisements.

A Visit to Ross-on-Wye means a Visit to

THE ROXY Luxury Cinema and Cafe

Perfect Entertainment

ONLY FIRST CLASS FILMS

●

*Fully Equipped for
Cinemascope, Vistavision
and
Wide Screen Presentations*

Continuous Daily from 5 p.m.,
Saturday from 2 p.m.
Sunday 7.30 p.m. only

Perfect Catering

FIRST CLASS CUISINE

●

*Fully Equipped for
Parties and Receptions*

Wide Selection of Dishes

**OPEN SEVEN DAYS
A WEEK**
From 10 a.m. to 10 p.m.

Proprietors : Ross Cinema and Theatre Co. Ltd.
General Manager : J. M. TOMMEY

**Phone 2398
DAY and NIGHT**

The Roxy Cinema in Broad Street opened its doors to the public on 6 April 1939. Its plush Art Deco style reflected its age of attractively packaged consumerism. It succumbed to the television age in the 1970s and now the Maltings shopping arcade covers much of this site.

Above: Most of the meat consumed in the town 100 years ago was produced locally, eliminating today's excessive food miles! The Probert brothers built up a thriving business selling beef, lamb and pork from their two shops at 1 Broad Street and 11 High Street in the centre of the town. The meat was from animals William Probert reared at Alton Court Farm. Staff and owners line up for G.W. Young's photograph advertising their Christmas fare outside their Broad Street shop in 1910. Sale hopes were high, especially as four of the carcasses carried notices reading 'Fed by His Majesty the King'.

Above left: This seemingly unremarkable anonymous postcard of Ross in 1930 shows how much this part of the town has changed in the latter half of the 20th century. Unfortunately only a few of the allotments in the foreground remain in cultivation from the original 55 at Cawdor Gardens. For years they were an important part of the economy of the families living nearby. In the 1960s new industrial buildings appeared on the corner of Trenchard and Greytree Roads and a tarmac-covered lorry and coach park covered the meadow to the right. About 1988 the cattle market was moved to the bypass and in 1990 the redundant railway embankment was bulldozed to provide gardens for the housing development in the aptly-named New Market Close. With long gardens facing the road most of the 30 houses in the Nursery fronted a sort of courtyard backing onto the railway embankment. The house on the left is one of the two pairs of original houses to survive demolition in the 1970s when the present smart houses with colourful gardens were built. Apparently unchanged, St. Mary's church on the top of the hill still dominates the scene as it has done for centuries.

CHAPTER TWO

The Church and the Prospect

Ross's charmingly irregular-shaped church was built in contemporary styles over three centuries. Work started on the nave and chancel about 1280, although the site, dedicated to St. Mary the Virgin, was undoubtedly used for a church much earlier than this. Windows in the chancel and aisles are evidence of this first phase. The tower was built in the early 14th century and work continued on and off until the south chapel was completed in 1510. The nave was rebuilt in 1745 using existing materials and has unusual banded pillars. The fabric of the church has been repaired, restored and rebuilt on several occasions, notably in 1862 when the bill topped £2,000, a sum including new pews. The east window in the chancel is noteworthy as it was bought cheaply from Stretton Sugwas and hastily installed, being eventually correctly reconstructed in 1873 by German glass experts who were then working at Wormelow.

The 208 ft. high spire was rebuilt under John Kyrle's supervision (and maybe with some of his money) in 1721. Repaired after a lightning strike in 1852, repaired again in 1911 and for a third time in 1952, it remains a landmark for miles around.

Prominently set above the town in a tree-filled churchyard, St. Mary's seems to be a changeless centre of a bustling town full of ever-changing life and growth. In the quiet interior, the Rudhall and

For centuries the church of St. Mary dominated the town of Ross until in 1837 James Barrett built the Royal and the Gazebo tower, changing the view for ever.

Westfaling monuments commemorate members of the rich and powerful families of the area. John Kyrle's tomb and a marble memorial, erected in 1764, 42 years after his death, are in the chancel. He was additionally commemorated in 1924 by the new church clock, which was installed to mark the bicentenary of his death on 11 November 1724. Affectionately remembered for his generosity to the town, one of his many gifts was a church bell in 1695. The present organ was a gift from Mrs. Purchas in 1921 to replace the original bought in 1826.

In 1910 an inspection revealed that the church tower urgently needed repairs. The usual appeal for funds followed and the Church Tower Fund slowly rose towards its target of £680, only £220 being on deposit at the bank in May 1911. Appeals during the summer raised enough money for work to proceed in September. It was then found that rebuilding work costing an additional £110 was required, necessitating yet more appeals for funds to cover the new estimate of £790.

Adjoining the churchyard to the north is the Prospect, which John Kyle was instrumental in designing in 1700. He leased the Prospect for 495 years to William Fisher, a farmer and the landlord of the nearby Pounds Inn, 'subject to a right for the inhabitants of Ross to walk therein'. Despite this, Fisher kept his pigs there, ruining Kyrle's work. By 1872 the Prospect was in good enough condition for a thousand people to sit down to a feast to celebrate the passing of the Reform Act through Parliament.

A timeless scene in the churchyard overlooked by St. Mary's elegant spire and the surrounding trees. So many Ross people lie buried in the churchyard that by 1908 the need for another burial ground was becoming acute. To overcome a controversial problem Mrs. Purchas bought Rectory Farm and donated two acres of land to the town to enlarge the churchyard. In thanking her for her generosity the mayor said 'The idea of a cemetery could sink into oblivion for another 50 years'. But the needs of an increasing population compelled the Ross on Wye Urban District Council to buy the land for the present cemetery at Tudorville on the outskirts of the town in 1940.

Above: St. Mary's parishioners regarded the unusual arrival of two elm root suckers beside John Kyrle's old pew as a good omen and allowed them to grow tall. By the end of the 19th century they had, of course, become tourist attractions and numerous photographs and postcards of them exist. The trees eventually succumbed to Dutch Elm disease in the 1970s and had to be removed. To continue the tradition, Russian vines have been planted to replace them. Note the superbly graceful ornate gas lamps which illuminated the scene on dark winter evenings.

Left: Eight men and a boy pose for R.E. Davies's camera during a pause in the repair work on the spire in October 1911. After removing the weathercock, the foreman steeplejack took his young son to the top of the spire, 208 feet above the ground for this photograph. For a heartstopping moment the lad stood, arms outstretched like a crucifix, and enjoyed a brief but unforgettable view over Ross as the camera clicked to record the moment. The weathercock was made from a 2 ft. square piece of gilded copper having been replaced in October 1852 following a lightning strike. In 1951, 40 years later, a Faculty was issued for repairing the top 25 feet of the spire; the work being carried out in 1952 at a cost of £1,300.

Above: In spite of the common belief in nearly 100% church attendance during Victorian times, census returns show that only a third of the population regularly attended Sunday services. A large, well-rehearsed choir added to everyone's enjoyment of the services, and the 36 members of St. Mary's church choir face Dickie Davies's camera for their 1905 photograph with their choirmaster and the Rector Edward Winnington-Ingram in the centre.

Right: Even in modern times disease can travel far and wide and is carried from country to country by travellers and traders. This was the way the plague travelled across Europe and England in the 17th century. Ross did not escape the 1637 outbreak despite the quarantine restrictions imposed at Wilton Bridge and probably other places. Inscribed on the plinth of the mediaeval preaching cross in the churchyard is a memorial to the 315 men, women and children of Ross who lost their lives in the epidemic and are buried in a mass grave nearby.

THE PLAGUE CROSS, ROSS.

Right: This delightful Edwardian postcard shows elegant ladies, well-behaved children and super-plush prams enjoying the 1908 spring sunshine in the Prospect.

Above and left: Old photographs of this part of Ross show sloping rocks below the Prospect before the new Wilton Road was cut. These views of the road in summer and winter give some idea of how quiet rural roads, even the main road to Hereford, were 100 years ago. The contrast with the busy scene this road presents today, especially at holiday weekends, is remarkable. Maybe the coach in Wye Street is a portent of its present popularity. The path up the side of the cliff leads to the ever popular John Kyrle's Walk.

PROSPECT, ROSS.

AT A
MEETING OF THE INHABITANTS

OF THE TOWN OF ROSS,

AND ITS NEIGHBOURHOOD, DULY CONVENED BY PUBLIC ADVERTISEMENT,

AND HELD

AT THE TOWN HALL,

ON TUESDAY the 3rd day of DECEMBER, 1839, for the purpose of considering the steps necessary to be taken to maintain and preserve the rights of the Public over the PROSPECT, threatened to be extinguished by

MR. BARRETT, THE PROPRIETOR OF THE ROYAL HOTEL, IN THAT TOWN.

Left: In 1839 a Public Meeting was held to discuss the public rights of access to the Propspect and the threats by Mr. Barrett of the Royal Hotel to extinguish them. There was much righteous indignation and a Committee was set up with a Subscription Fund to uphold the rights of the citizens of Ross to full access to the Prospect.

Above: An unusual view of Wilton Road looking towards the town when Caroline Symond's Gardens was still privately owned, divided from Wye Street by a hedge. The trees along Wilton Road had not yet been planted to obscure the view of Springfield Farm nestling in the trees at the top of the hill (centre left). Most of Springfield is now covered with modern housing and the barely visible allotments at Cawdor Gardens have all but disappeared. Only one car is visible on the road which is now so crowded with traffic that no-one can walk down the middle of it as the Edwardians could, without a care in the world. This entry to Ross past the man-made cliff is framed by the British and Foreign School built in 1837 and the Gazebo tower on the right. The whole photo encaspulates the slowly growing town of Ross; the by-passed Wye Street, the 1830s road and school improvements, Victorian gas street lighting, an early car and the altered skyline where small houses have now been enlarged with the housing expansion of the 20th century yet to come.

The big national, firms like Friths, Tucks & Valentines photographed the tourist spots of a town like Ross *ad nauseam*, so it was left to the local photographers, with time and local knowledge, to photograph and publish postcards of the lesser known places that townsfolk liked to visit.

These delightful views of John Kyrle's Walk through Little Wood were taken by H.E. Wilkins in 1908 and show how popular it was then. The boys look a little sad — maybe their girlfriends never turned up.

The Act was greeted as a momentous reform, allowing householders the vote and was the first step in the long process of enfranchising the whole adult population. Little did these citizens realise the imminent troubles with the Prospect. James Barrett bought the lease when he built the Royal Hotel in 1837 and laid out gardens solely for his customers to enjoy. It was these gardens that the enraged citizens of Ross destroyed when they rioted to reclaim the Prospect which they regarded as their own. The protests died down when, after Barrett's death, Thomas Blake quietly bought the Royal Hotel and grounds and installed a manageress. He later legally transferred the Prospect, at his own expense, to the townspeople for ever. John Kyrle's original gateways remain and the trees have matured, although the gardens have long gone. A pleasanter spot for a war memorial would be difficult to find, for the views beyond are still attractive despite the intervening bridge on the by-pass. The Prospect continues to attract a steady stream of people, most of them quite unaware of its unusual history.

In 1833 the New Road was cut below the Prospect into the side of the old red sandstone, forming a man-made cliff. The red dust which rose from passing traffic before the surface was sealed with tarmac together with the pink valerian and red wallflowers on the cliff in Spring soon led to it acquiring its local name — Red Hill. Now called Wilton Road, it was constructed during the turnpike era to avoid the old steep road up Wye Street and to give horse-drawn traffic a gentler and quicker approach to the town. Debris from the rocks removed was used to raise the height of the causeway approach to Wilton Bridge so as to be above the winter flood level.

CHAPTER THREE

Floods and the River Wye

The Wye has played an important part in the Ross economy for hundreds of years, providing a route for goods up and down the river and later for tourists to enjoy the scenery. In 1745, the year of Bonnie Prince Charlie's rebellion, Rev. John Egerton first started arranging boat trips for tourists to admire the scenery of the Wye Valley. By 1760 boats were hired in increasing numbers to the wealthy and famous. Pleasure boating remained popular for 150 years, but is now restricted to Ross Rowing Club, raft races and the occasional canoe.

Depending upon the season, thoughts of the river will probably engender either an idyllic sunny day sitting on the bank or in a boat, or wondering when the floodwaters might peak. However, matters may appear confused as in the image of August 1912 when the Tennis Club went underwater. Unfortunately for the tournament, organised by the South Herefordshire Lawn Tennis and Croquet Club at the Park and contested by nationally known players, the last week of August turned out to be disastrously rainy. At the end of a very wet summer, two inches fell on the first day, stopping play completely. On Tuesday a little play was possible on a few courts, but by Wednesday morning the players and organisers were greeted with a tide of brown floodwater from the Wye that covered the courts two feet deep. Four events had to be cancelled as play was removed to private courts at Weir End and Merryvale. Pictures of boating on the tennis court and other flood pictures were advertised at Beeston's Photographers in Broad Street on 29 August.

Well away from the river Wye, Brookend Street is famous locally for its floods, occasionally as a result of the Wye overflowing, but more often because the drains were overwhelmed by a large volume of rainwater. The drains back up discharging filthy water into the street. Even modern flood prevention schemes still seem unable to cope with prolonged heavy rain.

Floods like this one on 28 August 1912 usually only occur in the autumn and winter months. The tennis tournament was well interrupted and the mixed doubles pair of Miss Moody and Mr. Kingdom decided to enjoy the scenery of the tennis courts from a rowing boat instead.

Above: The flood of 28 August 1912 viewed from the Prospect over the roofscape of Wye Street. Without the trees now growing along the river bank from the Hope and Anchor to the rowing club the course of the Wye is completely obliterated by the height of the water. The terraced houses along Greytree Road stand out against the open fields of Springfield, now covered with houses. Further along the road was the town rubbish tip, which generated a flow of complaints from local residents for many years. Just visible as a white dot are the level crossing gates on the corner of Greytree road, now only a distant memory of part of the lost railway to Hereford. Only a few houses stand near the bottom of the hill near the railway line. The avenues of houses at Greytree were then only a planner's dream.

Right: In the same floods of 28 August 1912, Henry Dowell was forced to haul his rowing boats out of the water to the safety of dry land in front of the pub. The floating landing stage holds the remainder of his little fleet secure against the flood. In the distance a tent stands forlornly in the water near Wilton Bridge, while everyone wonders how much higher the waters will reach. Henry Dowell measured 14 ft. of flood water at the dock.

Top: Photographed on a hot still sunny afternoon the *Wilton Castle* heads upstream with a party of 20 people and a crew of two. Henry Dowell, the owner, steers from a position in the stern just in front of the paddle wheels. Note the bracket for holding the funnel when lowered for negotiating Wilton Bridge, and also the framework for holding a canvas canopy to protect passengers from the rain and sun which could be very hot on the river.

Bottom: A close study of these two photographs reveals that fairly soon after its commissioning, the *Wilton Castle* was altered to improve the skipper's visibility and steering position, probably during the winter of 1902/03. The stern-steering position was too awkward as the funnel and engine room obscured the view forward. Mr. Dowell modified his new launch by moving the wheel in front of the funnel. He also provided a second awning for the passengers in the bows. A new coat of paint and two black bands on the top of the funnel made the smoke stain less noticeable and completed the overhaul. This stern-wheel paddle boat design is believed to be unique on British rivers. After ten years of use the *Wilton Castle* was moored in 1912 and slowly rotted away on the river bank due to wartime conditions when boating lost its appeal.

The 1947 winter remains in the national memory for its period of prolonged snowfall — but it had to melt at some stage! Eventually in late March it thawed, resulting in widespread serious flooding. Ross suffered along with the rest of the country with the water in Brookend Street so deep that people had to be rescued by boat. The flood water was so strong that Strangford Bridge on the railway line from Ross to Hereford was washed away. Railway services were suspended as stations like Kerne Bridge flooded completely, with water in the offices and waiting rooms.

Some 45 years earlier, to meet people's increasing calls for excursion trips for large parties on the river, Henry Dowell designed and built the *Wilton Castle* and eventually launched it. But this was not the first steam beat built in the town. The *Ross Gazette* reported in August 1874 that Hobbs and Dowell had built a steam launch at the dock beside the Hope and Anchor Inn for Captain Pryce Hamilton Esq. of Wilton House. It completed a satisfactory trial trip on Monday 20 August 1874 with 'six passengers, the owner and a smart boy'. Mrs. Hamilton steered it 'round the cranks and crooks of the Wye' at a speed of 8 m.p.h. generated by its screw propeller.

According to a report in the *Ross Gazette* on 29 May 1902, Henry Dowell had finished work on the *Wilton Castle* — a steam launch of his own design based on his local knowledge of the Wye. Work had been delayed for two years because Sisson & Co. of Gloucester were unable to guarantee delivery of the engine due to the Boer War and an engineers' strike. It was not until Thursday 15 May 1902 that a free trial trip was enjoyed by 106 people in what was certainly the first stern-wheel paddle-steamer in Britain passed by the Board of Trade.

The *Wilton Castle* was 65ft. long with a beam of 10ft. on a flat bottom drawing only 13 or 14 inches of water. It was oak-framed and planked with deal and pitch pine. Its compact engine consisted of a compound jet condenser delivering 25 h.p., fed from a marine-type boiler working at 95lbs. pressure. The 6ft. 8ins. diameter paddle-wheels spun at 60 revs. per minute pushing her along at 8 m.p.h. Complete with seating for 100 people, awnings and four lifebelts it cost Henry Dowell £700. An hour's trip cost 6d. and a return trip to Goodrich 1s. It was moored at Henry Dowell's dock at the Hope and Anchor Inn, 'formerly the dock for the old packet which in times gone by brought nearly all the freight to the Town'.

An advertisement in April 1903 read 'The *Wilton Castle* launch, Licensed by the Board of Trade, for a trip to Hole in the Wall on Sunday at 3p.m. First Class passengers 1s. 6d., second class 1s.' It continued giving pleasure trips on the Wye for some ten years. On 8 September 1904, for instance, the Ross Volunteers held a picnic at Backney Common for 200 members, families and friends. The *Wilton Castle* had to make two trips, heavily laden with 100 people each journey, to transport everyone there. On another occasion the officers of the Staffordshire Regiment in camp at Hildersley chartered it for an afternoon trip to Lydbrook.

A man positioned in the stern held a long quant pole in case the boat got into difficulty on an unseen shoal. This was not an uncommon occurrence as the water level in the river could vary considerably from day to day.

Thomas Henry Dowell's Hope and Anchor pub has changed little since this 1910 photograph by Henry Palmer, with the Royal Hotel, St. Mary's church and the Gazebo tower dominating the skyline. The Wye flows at its low summer level and only one rowing boat is hauled up on the bank. The line of rowing; boats moored to the floating pontoon are a reminder of how popular boating on the river used to be for tourists and townspeople alike.

It is said that if the man with the pole failed to shift the launch, Henry Dowell would ask the young men to jump out and push!

Henry Dowell was also landlord of the Hope and Anchor Inn, where a ferry boat took people across the river during busy times in Edwardian and Victorian days. Dowell also ran a basket-making business at the dock beside the pub and in January 1930, in an attempt to boost trade as the number of unemployed in Ross rose to over 250, he placed this advertisement in the *Ross Gazette*:

> T.H. Dowell est. over 100 years.
> Manufacturer of Baskets Skips and Hampers
> All Kinds of Wickerwork
> Every kind of Basket made to order
> Repairs promptly executed
> All kinds of chairs reseated
> Cane seats Rush seats Wicker seats
> Garden Chairs and Tables
> Support Home Industry

Even this apparently quiet business had its dangers. In 1912 two men bringing a punt fully laden with withies from Wilton capsized opposite the Hope and Anchor and nearly drowned, only being rescued with great difficulty.

For many years a regatta was held on the Wye at Ross. A report of water sports and watermen's rowing races at the regatta course on 18 July 1876 describes a coracle race with at least four entries. The men paddled their coracles from the Hope and Anchor to the withy beds at Wilton, from where they had to carry their craft across

Left top: Thirty-four members of Ross Rowing Club pose with crossed oars and their trophies at the end of the 1906 season. Their regular training sessions on Monday and Friday evenings must have then seemed well worth while. Their 1905 season had ended with a financial deficit of £5 as the club had bought a new boat for 22 guineas and subscriptions had to be raised from 10s. to 15s. to cover the deficit and put the club back on a sound financial footing.

Left bottom: The 1909 organising committee superintend their annual regatta from a small tent beside their new boathouse. This had been officially opened on Tuesday 14 July 1908.

Top: Children splash in the shallows to cool off in an interval in the regatta programme while the crowd awaits more racing.

Bottom left: A coxed four on the Wye pose for Dickie Davies's camera in front of the Rope Walk with the *Wilton Castle* moored to the river bank.

Bottom right: Auntie Hattie sent this delightful postcard of herself, Nancie, Harry and cousin Miriam, not forgetting Nancie's dog, home to Sheffield after a visit to Ross in July 1911 where they all enjoyed a picnic after punting up the river past the boathouse on a hot summer afternoon.

the fields to the river by the stream and then paddle downstream to the winning line at the Hope and Anchor and a much needed pint of refreshment. The *Ross Gazette* for 9 August 1906 includes a long list of the rowing races at that year's regatta including, surprisingly, swimming and diving events and again a coracle race. As dusk fell, illuminated boats, led by the *Wilton Castle*, sailed up and down the river to the music of Ross Town Band, and the whole scene was lit by a tremendous firework display. A joint collection for the club and the hospital raised funds for each, giving the President, H. Child, and the Secretary/Treasurer, J. Pencombe, plenty of satisfaction for their day's work.

Top: Brookend Street is famous locally for its floods, occasionally as a result of the Wye overflowing, but more often because the drains back up, discharging filthy water into the street. Even modern flood prevention schemes seem unable to cope with prolonged, heavy rain.

A group of interested workmen stop their bicycles to see the effects of just such a flood on 20 June 1936. The depth of the flood water can be seen by the mark on the wall on the right. The Barrel Inn was flooded 6ins. deep in dirty water and sewage. On the left, Blakes' second hardware store was later taken down to give an entry to the swimming pool car park. Butcher's petrol pumps were sited on the pavement for the convenience of motorists and can just be seen beyond the crowd. William Langford's dining rooms were once renowned for their meals, although Kelly's 1937 directory listed it as a grocery shop. As the floods receded temporary boards gave customers dry access to the shops.

Bottom: On the corner of Station Street a policeman watches as two rescuers push some residents of Brookend Street to safety on dry land in a small rowing boat. This scene in March 1947 was repeated in December 2000 and with the predicted weather changes due to global warming could easily be seen again without proper flood control for the area. Cleaning up the effects of this filthy flood water took months of work.

Top left: Winter 1947 is remembered for its prolonged. heavy snowfalls. Widespread flooding followed the thaw in the middle of March and by 20 March the Wye had flooded up to the bottom of Wye Street and surrounded the Riverside Restaurant. This is not immediately recognisable as the chimneys on the gable end have been removed, the wall and trees have gone and the front opened up to the road, altering the appearance of the building considerably. During a period when many pubs have closed, this restaurant changed its status to a public house in 1999. Renamed the Riverside Inn, it is now a popular addition to the Ross waterfront.

Bottom left: This R.E. Davies photograph shows how badly the Rudhall Brook could flood after prolonged heavy rainfall. Undated, but probably about 1912, these half submerged tree trunks lay in Broad Meadows immediately behind the station. Just above the flood water beyond the pollarded willows on the far side of the meadows stands Ross Tannery.

Ross Rowing Club realised it needed its own premises beside the river and after some energetic fund raising they had enough to start the building work themselves in late winter 1908. By Easter it was near enough finished for the club to move in after installing the town's mains water themselves. Ten shilling shares at 5% interest were offered to the public to help raise the remainder of the £290 needed, although members' own money was preferred. At the 1908 A.G.M. membership was opened to ladies on equal terms to men. The Club organised an annual regatta and that for 1908 proved to be the best they had held so far, with crews from Penarth, Cardiff, Worcester, Gloucester, Derby, Evesham and Stratford taking part. Captain Clive M.P. congratulated them on their 'beautiful new boat house' which was the venue for an outdoor dance in the evening finished off with a firework display on land and on the river. C. Footitt, the joint secretary, reported on the 1908 season as the best ever, with the biggest regatta, a balance at the bank and a 'good fleet of racing and pleasure boats'.

CHAPTER FOUR

'There weren't any Slums in Ross'

Owing to changes in the economic climate during and after the Napoleonic Wars people were drawn to towns in search of work. Ross, like others, started to expand. An 1822 map shows new houses in Overross and Brampton Streets, but rising interest rates at the time, higher building costs, and a scarcity of good-quality building materials resulted in badly-built houses. Within a short time they deteriorated into slums which took most of the 20th century to clear. The speculatively built terraces of the 1830s were scarcely any better. The word slum derives from 'slump' meaning literally 'to slip down into the mud', but also 'a marshy place' or 'a wet mire' and was first coined in the 1820s to describe dirty, damp, working-class houses in industrial areas that were often built on wet, marshy places.

As early as 1912 bad housing conditions were reported by Ross's Sanitary Inspector who complained of overcrowded and dilapidated properties and recommended repairs to houses in Brampton, Millpond and Wye Streets. However, there was no accommodation available for families whilst thorough repairs to their houses were being carried out. Whilst the Union Workhouse was usually only half occupied, unhelpful regulations prevented admissions from people unless they were actually homeless. As a result people were forced to continue living in hundred-year-old, poor, damp, overcrowded, badly-ventilated houses, often with no garden and sharing inadequate toilet facilities, with no foreseeable chance of improvement.

Six months before the end of the First World War in March 1918, Ross Urban District Council considered the need for the 'provision of houses for the working class' and discussed a rehousing scheme that would be financed by Local Government loans and a 75% Government grant. The urgent need for new housing had been revealed following repeated inspections under the provisions of the Housing and Planning Act of 1909, which gave councils power to inspect, improve, close, demolish and rebuild uninhabitable houses. Of 250 houses inspected in Ross in 1913, 100 required immediate repairs. Owners carried out cheap, unsatisfactory repairs to 33 of these, but as a whole the owners regarded houses as an investment not needing any re-investment because the lack of other available housing kept the rents up. The serious homelessness of the times is revealed by the Sanitary Inspector's report on lodging houses in Ross. That same year of 1913, despite the squalid conditions, 27,463 nights of accommodation were provided in four lodging houses in the town (averaging some 17 per lodging house per night). Most related to tramps in search of work, but some represented homeless families who eventually ended up in the Union Workhouse. Numbers in the 1920s were little less, when rising unemployment forced people to travel in search of work.

Although people remember the camaraderie and willingness to help each other, the squalid reality of their lives in such accommodation is something that should not be forgotten. Sixty-three people living beside the railway in Overross shared one lavatory, whilst very poor drains and in some houses even a lack of cooking stoves added to the misery. Just one example of the dilapidation of these old houses was the collapse of the back wall of No. 24 Edde Cross Street in July 1930. It fell on a four-year-old girl breaking her wrist so badly that despite Dr. Dunlop's best efforts at Ross Cottage Hospital he was unable to prevent permanent damage to her arm. Conditions in the street were just as bad. In 1915 a three-year-old boy fell 3 feet off the raised pavement in Brampton Street, hit his head and died in hospital; the Council could not erect a protective fence through lack of funds. (Even now this has not been completely fenced).

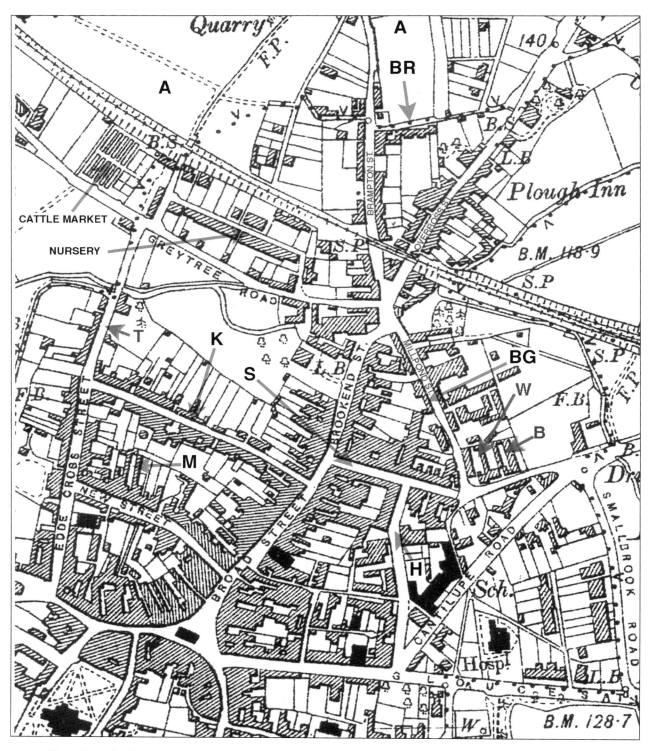

T — Trenchard	K — Kyrle Street	BG — Batts Gardens
W — Wolverhampton Terrace	M — Morley Square	BR — Brookfield Road
B — Broadmead Terrace	H — Henry Street	Reproduced from the 1906
S — Station Street	A — Allotments	Ordnance Survey map

44

For many years the Police Station was situated off Greytree Road behind the Friends' Meeting House. From there Superintendent Broad, who also lived in a substandard house, must have been very aware of the everyday lives of the people in Brampton Street when describing it as 'the poorest, most poverty-stricken street in Ross'. As well as describing the companionship, love and comradeship to be found there, John Griffiths in *From Brampton Street to Harwell* also mentioned its 'abject poverty in the wealthiest of nations [where] all the children went barefoot'. These contemporary accounts, as well as the Sanitary Inspector's reports, provide an impression of the conditions that the inhabitants of the 50 or more cottages, crammed between the railway viaduct and Brookfield Road, had to endure. Better off parents even warned their children 'not to play in Brampton Street'. Other poor streets were regarded as virtual 'no go' areas for outsiders. Older residents can still remember children from the slum areas going to school in the 1930s in very ragged clothes and worn out shoes. 'No shoes' was an excuse frequently used to explain absence from school. Brenda Smith remembers taking second-hand clothes and shoes to school for some of these unfortunate children to wear.

'Homes fit for Heroes' was the politicians' slogan for the benefit of the thousands of returning servicemen, but like most slogans, it was to prove difficult to fulfill. A week after the armistice, on 18 November 1918, the Council accepted that rehousing should be regarded as 'a matter of extreme urgency in view of the approaching demobilisation' of servicemen. Yet only two weeks later they rejected a joint report from A.H. Pearson, the Surveyor, and Frank Ricketts, the Sanitary Inspector, calling for 169 new, low-rent houses. Had this report been accepted and fully acted upon when government grants were available, many of their future problems and delays would have been avoided and many lives improved. A year later, on 31 October 1919, another detailed report by their Medical Officer of Health and the Sanitary Inspector listed 89 houses as being unfit for human habitation and 27 below standard, affecting 324 inhabitants in Brampton, New, Kyrle, and Edde Cross Streets, Old Gloucester Road, the Nursery and Overross.

Over time, the Council started to issue demolition orders on some of the properties in Brampton Street. Nine houses, completely unfit for habitation at Batt's Gardens in Millpond Street, were demolished in 1920 at a cost of £68 15s., with the intention of providing a children's recreation ground. The standard of fitness then required of homes to be declared fit for habitation included freedom from dampness, satisfactory lighting and ventilation, proper drainage and sanitary conveniences with a satisfactory water supply, adequate washing accommodation, and adequate facilities for cooking and storing food in a well-ventilated food store.

But it was the first national conference of Sanitary Inspectors in Birmingham in November 1919 that saw a turning point for council housing, for the inspectors, employed by the District Councils, were the key officials in reporting on bad housing and recommending the new houses that were required as a result. The Housing of the Working Classes Act passed earlier that year had given powers to District Councils, such as the then Ross Urban District Council, for financing local government housing schemes. Greenfield sites were favoured for new developments in Ross as in most small towns, for it was easier and more economic to provide new services to a large number of houses on 'clean' land as opposed to piecemeal redevelopments among existing houses.

A site at Archenfield was identified as suitable for some of the desperately needed houses, but local householders did not want working class houses anywhere near their expensive dwellings. It took two years of discussion and dissension before a site at Duxmere was finally purchased and work started on 28 February 1921 on a first phase of 36 three-bedroomed houses. Local men were employed on site as far as possible so as to remove some from the dole queues. During the period of construction the builder's foreman complained that he was continually interrupted in his work by local people inquiring when the houses would be ready and what the rents would be. The Duxmere site was renamed Red Hill in February 1922 when the first tenants moved in at a weekly rent of 7s. 6d. A little later in 1924, instead of a children's playground in Millpond Street, four two-bedroomed houses, costing £1,804 were built under a new Housing Act of 1923. Here the rent was 11s. a week to include urban, water and poor rates.

After this date Government money was no longer available and, despite the Urban District Council's appeals, no grants for new housing were forthcoming. Councillors were unwilling to sanction big increases in the rates to build more houses in Ross to alleviate the problems, which were now worsening due to increasing unemployment. The official figures gave 248 men and 38 women out of work in 1931, but unofficially there were many more. Frank Owen, the local Liberal M.P., certainly knew what he was talking about when he said in a speech in 1930: 'Even in Ross there are appalling slums'. For its size the social housing problems in Ross were just as great as those in Hereford where 1,000 council houses were built between the two World Wars.

Another government scheme provided a subsidy to private builders, and in 1924 one local builder erected a house for rent which qualified under the scheme for a subsidy of £75 16s., only to have this meagre amount reduced to £50 6s. two years later. This was hardly an incentive for private landlords when the house cost £700 to build, and the expected rent was between £20 and £25 *per annum*. Generally speaking owners were reluctant to spend money on their substandard properties.

Although another four houses were built at Red Hill, the Sanitary Inspector's reports for 1925 and '26 make depressing reading — 15% of all houses inspected were unfit for human habitation, and only 12 had been repaired. Overcrowding was also becoming more of a problem; in one case 19 people shared a two-roomed cottage. It took over two years for the Sanitary Inspector to persuade the landlord of a row of cottages in Millpond Street to repair the leaking roof and install flush toilets. Owners also failed to comply with the Council's closure orders despite repeated pressure. The Council proposed a plan for 100 houses in 1928 which lapsed as government funds simply were not available.

Of 83 houses inspected in 1930, 21 were unsuitable and a further 17 completely unfit for human habitation, but there was no suitable alternative accommodation to house the families concerned. Tenants unfortunate enough to live in such circumstances were thus unable realistically to speak up and complain about their appalling living conditions as they had nowhere else to go and the rents of 5s. to 10s. weekly were exorbitant.

In November 1930 a Mr. Braby offered the Council 4½ acres of land at the back of the cattle market for free on which to build council housing. He also offered to build five cottages to rehouse slum dwellers at affordable rents of 5s. or 6s. weekly if the Council renovated or demolished a similar number of cottages. Initially interested in the idea, the Council turned down the proposal in January 1931 as the land was only available if the Council constructed a sewer and access road to the five planned cottages. By this time Ross Urban District Council had its own plans to build at Brampton Road, Tudorville, Camp Road and Overross.

It was in 1930 that the Government finally recognised the problem that existed nationwide and passed a Housing Act that gave local Councils the responsibility for slum clearance and rehousing and provided the funds to carry out the work. There was also the added intention to inject some finance into local economies to remove some of the unemployed from the dole queues. The Government thus restored subsidies that enabled Councils to build houses at cheap rents for the disadvantaged and poorly paid 'as private enterprise is failing to provide for them'. Under the Act the Sanitary Committee could either recommend a closing order be made if a dwelling was found to be in bad repair and unfit for human habitation, or issue a repair and improvement notice that required renovations to be commenced within 28 days.

Taking advantage of this Act, Ross on Wye Urban District Council started to issue closure orders on houses deemed unfit and in May 1932 bought 2½ acres of land at the top of Brampton Street for £375 'for working class dwellings'. The Public Loans Board was approached for finance, that would be repaid over a 40 year period, to build 24 houses not exceeding 760 square feet floor area to be let at 7s. per week. Messrs. Cutter and Sysum of Ledbury offered the lowest quote at £310 per house. They subsequently had to lower the figure to £303 by using cheaper bricks and tiles, saving the ratepayers a reported total of £98 (*sic*). Building work started on 28 November before the contracts were formally signed on a revised plan

The six houses constituting Wolverhampton Terrace were in Millpond Street with their backyards and sheds where Morrisons petrol filling station now stands. Frank Ricketts, the Sanitary Inspector, reported in August 1933: 'Floors rough flag stones, rooms dark, windows small, ventilation bad, some damp here and there, ceilings bulging in places. Some of these houses are particularly well cared for by the tenants so that the defects in the walls are masked. Common yard at back rough. One standpipe for water, and one drain only for all spoutings, down pipes and drainage are all inadequate. Wash house, coal shed and lavatory are in one shed at top of yard. No flush, no privacy. Houses could be reconditioned but it would be better to build three new cottages'.

Appearances were deceptive as Marion Willavoys (née Preston) said that from a child's point of view they appeared to be pleasant houses from the outside. When she played there with a friend the houses seemed attractive, but she did not live there or know the whole story.

for 32 houses, eight for selected tenants from overcrowded properties and 24 to rehouse slum dwellers. The workforce included as many local men as possible. Completed in May 1933, the houses were let at 5s. 7d. and 6s. weekly. The Council declined to build garden sheds as they would have cost an extra £100 and would have added 2d. to the weekly rent.

The Rent Restriction Act of 1933 prevented landlords of slum property increasing the rent if the tenant could produce a certificate from the Sanitary Authority (ie the District Council) that the house was not in a reasonable state of repair. Whilst this protected tenants financially, it proved to be another disincentive to landlords to spend money to upgrade poor property with little prospect of increased profit.

On 28 May 1933 Ross on Wye Urban District Council finally adopted a Five Year Plan for slum clearance in the town presented by Dr. Haine, the Medical Officer of Health. He reported that

> It was absolutely necessary because of the progressive dilapidation of the housing and the increasing congestion of the population. Housing was the chief and most urgent problem for the Local Authority who should immediately embark upon a progressive and complete programme [for rehousing] as the problem affects not only the welfare of the town but the health of the inhabitants individually.

The main reasons that clearance was deemed to be the most appropriate solution were listed as sanitary defects and general disrepair.

On 5 February 1934 the Council repeated its adoption of the Five Year Plan, designating three clearance areas. Area No 1 was Brampton Street where 43 houses were inhabited by 194 people. This area was to be dealt with first, using the houses built at the top of Brampton Street as a start to the rehousing programme. Edde Cross Street was designated as Area No 2, its 30 houses and 70 inhabitants to be dealt with in the light of experience gained from Area No. 1. This was the biggest area and it was felt that 'a sweeping clearance would benefit the town'. Millpond Street was designated as Area No. 3, 'the smallest and least urgent, if it is possible to speak in relative terms of unhealthy houses'. Seventy people lived in the 18 affected houses in this area. Further clearance orders in August covered four houses in Alton Street, and nine in Gloucester Road.

Notice was also given under the Town and Country Planning Act of 1932 that anyone wishing to build, rebuild or develop subsequent to the demolition orders must obtain Council permission first. Plans would have to be submitted if owners wished to renovate or reconstruct properties with a demolition order on them, and this could be done before the Inquiry into the clearance orders scheduled for November. Owners were also reminded that the properties could not be retained for use as stores, which was a way the owners thought they might be able to circumvent the orders.

In a report by Dr. Haine on houses that could be reconditioned by their owners he wrote:

> Notice how persistently we return to the Brampton Street district as the part of Ross where most improvements are required, and it can be brought about. A bold policy is called for and if the whole area is made an Improvement Area [essentially a clearance area, under the Housing Act of 1930] including good, bad and repairable houses I am sure that we shall complete most rapidly and effectively a notable improvement to the town of Ross that will be of permanent value. It would be up to owners to decide their course of action, whether to recondition, demolish or appeal to the courts. 'This was a genuine effort by the Council to raise the standard of living in Ross. People should not look at it in money values alone but realise they were providing healthy comfortable houses for people to live in.

Dr. Haine's report told of 104 houses and 443 people affected, and detailed the defects in each building. Accepting his report, the Council stated that it intended building 70 houses at Tudorville and 30 more on suitable demolition sites to house displaced families. The effect on Ross on Wye was enormous as 10% of the population of 4,720 (as indicated by the 1931 census) would move to homes on the outskirts of the town. The Council duly informed the Ministry of Health of its plans, and in his last report before moving on to another job in May 1934, Dr. Haine was able to say:

These 11 houses in Broadmead Terrace stood parallel to Wolverhampton Terrace at right angles to Station Street on what is now Morrisons roadway, between the car park and filling station. Kemp's woodyard and chimney are apparent beyond the houses and Llewellyn's corrugated iron shed stands on the right. The Sanitary Inspector's report was very similar to that for Wolverhampton Terrace except that he noted that the ceilings were higher. A single pump supplied well water to all 11 houses. There was no piped water. These houses would have been very expensive to recondition and demolition was considered to be the only solution. Despite their poor surroundings people tried to better themselves. Working at his home at 11 Broadmead Terrace H. Pullen became well-known locally for the quality of his boot and shoe repairs.

The health of the town has never been better and there has been freedom from all epidemics. The housing programme is complete on paper, there should be no other than small technical difficulties in its way. I trust the council will proceed energetically and complete the permanent elimination of all slum property.

Reporting on the individual houses designated in the clearance areas Mr. Ricketts, the Sanitary Inspector, commented:

They were not really viable to patch up on a piecemeal basis. Rents for dilapidated properties were above [those for] council houses, which provided better facilities. Some hovels' rents were 8s. or 10s. weekly. Rents for slums varied enormously with unhealthy conditions, bad lighting, bad ventilation and defective sanitary arrangements in the widest sense.

At a special meeting on 8 November 1934 the Urban District Council awarded M. Wilesmith of Malvern Link a contract to build 42 houses at Tudorville for £13,110 (roughly £312 per house). This was the first phase of development on land bought earlier for £565. In January, Wilesmith submitted another quote to build the remaining 28 houses for £8,750, which was confirmed on 22 January. Ross Water Undertaking quoted £197 9s. 2d. for connecting the water supply, and William F. Rees Ltd. commenced work on the roads and sewers on the estate in February at a contracted price of £1,873 10s. 2d. All these contracts met with the Ministry of Health's full approval.

It was essential to complete houses for the occupants of the clearance areas well before demolition work began and, although there was a shortage of skilled bricklayers, building work progressed satisfactorily, allowing houses to be ready when needed. In October 1936 the new houses at Tudorville were completed to the Council's satisfaction, apart from a few minor defects which the contractor was to rectify. In addition, five allotments on some spare ground were marked out for tenants at 5s. annual rent, whilst eight new gas lamps costing £48 18s. 6d. lit the streets. Tenants from Brampton Street were offered the first houses, and all accepted the offer readily at rents of 6s. 6d.

Allied to the various new housing schemes was the realisation that the town's sewers were both antiquated and inadequate. The Council had procrastinated over this problem since 1900 as councillors saw no harm in discharging raw sewage directly into the Wye. But with the extra houses came the pressing need to improve the old system, especially as the County Council became more and more concerned about the pollution of the river. Various sewage schemes, costing between £7,000 and £30,000 (huge amounts for a town the size of Ross), were discussed and experts consulted to resolve the sewage problem.

In rural areas and on the fringes of urban areas some houses could be brought up to a reasonable standard using a subsidy system provided by the Rural Workers Housing Acts of 1926 and 1930. Ross and Whitchurch Rural District Council used the provisions of this Act, which provided for grant aid of between £50 and £100 for renovating decrepit agricultural workers' houses with improvements to the structure, water supply and drainage, but not for maintenance. The owner was expected to make up any difference in cost, but was not allowed to charge more than 4s. a week rent to his farm workers. Property owners were very slow to take up this offer of subsidies to improve their workers' houses, for there was no immediate financial gain in spending any money on improving cottages that could not be sold. By 1933 only 15 out of 99 eligible owners had applied. The position improved in 1934 with the Council spending £2,675 in subsidies on 33 cottages with another 30 to be considered the following year. Ross and Whitchurch Council eventually assisted with grants and loans in reconditioning 72 dilapidated cottages during a six year period, as compared with 46 in Ledbury, 25 in Dore, four in Hereford, one in Weobley and none at all in Bromyard, Leominster and Kington District Council areas.

As Ross on Wye U.D.C. preferred demolition, the Council laid down stringent criteria for repairs, as listed by Dr. Leo Foy, Dr. Haine's successor as Medical Officer of Health in 1935, and relating to meeting the standards that would enable properties to be declared fit for habitation:

Looking at them today no-one would know that these two cottages at 13 and 14 Alton Street had been recommended for demolition. The report said 'These two stone cottages are situated at the lower part of Alton Street. No. 13 consists of living room, parlour and two bedrooms. No. 14 is somewhat larger with living room, parlour, annexed scullery and three bedrooms. In No. 13 the ground floor ceilings were 6ft. 5ins., the bedrooms 7ft. 6ins. Lower floors are out of plane. Parlour wall is covered with canvas and papered over to mask dampness and defects. Kitchen is rather dark. Bedroom windows are undersize and one ceiling is precarious. Cellar in bare rock is damp with bad steps. Wash house walls are rough, roof defective and clothes boiler out of order. Outside steps defective. No provision for food storage which is kept on the cellar steps. Outside drain and water supply is 40ft. away'. In No. 14 the ceiling heights varied: 'kitchen 6ft. 7ins., annexed scullery 9ft., parlour 6ft. 11ins., bedrooms 7ft. and 7ft. 10ins. Windows undersize except one in the parlour. Ground floor very damp. Kitchen and parlour floorboards uneven and shaky. Bedroom ceilings bulged, walls damp. Roof above is in extremely bad condition. Dark staircase. Water tap in old wash house 40ft. from house with privy closets. Neither house has a damp course. The pantile roof is in very poor condition. It rains in. Walls crumbling, spouting missing These houses are occupied by four adults and are unfit for habitation.'

1. Site
   a) Suitable elevation. Low marshland was not suitable.
   b) Free circulation of air on two sides. Excavation of slopes if necessary. Paths to be surfaced and drained.
2. Outbuildings must not interfere with light and ventilation.
3. Lavatories. All must be flushed with mains water, be within reasonable distance and preferably under cover.
4. Water supply. Each house must have inside mains water.
5. Structure. Must be impervious to rain, a damp course where necessary. All roofs, gutterings and flashings to be in good repair.
6. Lighting. Adequate natural lighting for every room. Windows to be 10% of floor area.
7. Ventilation for every room with air vent if there was no fireplace. Half the window space to open.
8. Floor space. No bedroom to be less than 65 square feet.
9. Height of rooms to be a minimum 7 feet 6 inches.
10. Each house to have an adequate ventilated larder, a scullery with a sink, adequate cupboards and fuel store. All habitable rooms on ground floor to have a fireplace and one bedroom must also have a fireplace. There must be adequate cooking facilities. All surfaces were to be even and capable of easy cleaning—ie floors, walls, ceilings and external approaches.
11. Drainage. Each house to have adequate drainage system and a receptacle for refuse.

A variety of aspects of public health occupied different committees of the Ross on Wye Urban District Council during this decade. It was announced in 1935 that all the houses in Ross on Wye were supplied with water from the artesian wells at Alton Court, which had been tested and found to be completely satisfactory. The Water Company complained, however, that if the new council houses at Brampton Road had been designed with 100 gallon water storage tanks then their supply would have been sufficient and the larger new mains supply would not have been needed.

Meanwhile, new public conveniences, built by J. Robbins of Weston under Penyard at a cost of £1,150 were opened in Crofts Lane on 7 September 1935. Not everyone appreciated them, sad to say, and children soon started to vandalise them; three girls caused 7s. 6d. damage to some tiles within a fortnight of opening.

All these public health initiatives, large and small, were of great importance to Ross on Wye. Yet they seem to have provoked little local comment in the press or at public or Council meetings. What did, however, provoke many a lively debate was the question of whether or not to allow tennis to be played on Sundays on the new hard courts at Crossville. These had just been laid, had a very hard wearing and true finish designed to please both locals and to attract visitors and to make a profit for the town. The discussions centred on whether players would disturb services at St. Mary's and whether such recreation was sanctioned by the Bible.

Most landlords had opposed the Council's efforts to improve their tenants' housing for some 20 years and they remained determined to oppose the Council's will. They had the legal right to resist the demolition orders that the Council served on them because of the serious financial issues involved, and two inquiries had to be held before the clearance orders could be confirmed.

The first, in September 1934, concerned area No. 3, which covered properties in and around Millpond Street and Old Gloucester Road, and was held before a Ministry of Health Inspector. Mr. Brown, the owner of Broadmead Terrace said the terrace had cost him £1,100 to purchase and yielded an annual rent of £156. He had an estimate of £825 to put them in order and had offered the Council his plans two years ago, but had heard nothing until the demolition orders were served. He argued that a large Council shed cut out light and air in front of his houses, which were otherwise in a good position, and that he was unable to install sewerage until the Council installed a sewer. He had installed a piped water supply when the well became contaminated. Mrs. Brown and Mr. Clift stated their tenants in Wolverhampton Terrace were very well satisfied with their accommodation; one had lived there for 18 years and another for 35 years with no complaints. Mr. Dekin, the owner of Nos. 22–27 Old Gloucester Road, wished to retain these properties as stores for his antique furniture business.

These six cottages, owned by Mr. Bliss, stood in Kyrle Street, nearly opposite the back of the present Jaqueline's night club. Behind them was the gas works chimney and gasometer. On 11 April 1935 it was reported that four of them stood on the street front and the other two, Nos. 33 and 34, at the rear, were approached through a 3ft. 6ins. wide passageway (the last doorway in the row) — an example of poor planning and most inconvenient. They each had one room on the ground floor and two very small bedrooms.

All the usual defects were apparent: lack of food stores, sculleries, sinks and indoor water supply, and the presence of bad and defective floors, walls, ceilings, staircases, small windows, low ceilings, defective roofs and spouting and crumbling walls, with a communal wash house and one WC for the four cottages and one for the other two families. There were no drains, so slops were thrown into the road gully. The floors of Nos. 29 and 30 were 2ft. 8ins. below ground level. There was no back door and all were considered as of 'back-to-back' construction. A strip of land had been split into six gardens. Although there were 33 people living in these six cottages, only four were considered to be overcrowded. Clearance was ordered on 14 December 1933.

In response Mr. Ricketts, the Sanitary Inspector, stated that the houses in Broadmead Terrace were over 100 years old and had no damp course. As a result, they suffered from creeping damp, with fungi growing on the walls and water visible through the broken floors. Three tenants were eventually able to have their voices heard and gave witness that their homes were not fit to live in as they were overrun with beetles, cockroaches, mice, rats and fungus. After a six-hour hearing the Inspector said he would visit all the affected premises with their owners or agents and his decision would be notified soon.

Some of the landlords who were present at the first inquiry into area No. 3 had similar properties examined at the second inquiry into areas Nos. 1 and 2, chaired by Mr. N. Boothroyd. He listened to their objections against demolition orders on 26 November 1934 at Ross on Wye Police Court. The Council was represented by Hedley Watts, their clerk, Leo Foy, the Medical Officer of Health, and Frank Ricketts, the Sanitary Inspector. Objecting to the orders were the executors of the late Mr. G. Lewis, E. Dekin, the trustees of F. M. Matthews and the following people: M. Brown, S. Clift, Mrs. Davies, Mrs. Hodges, Mr. Bird, Dr. Cam, Mrs. Arnold, A.J. Dean and Mr. Lock.

It was stated for the Council that the houses in the 17 clearance areas, which were the subject of this inquiry, were much below standard and that their deficiency demanded demolition. However, the Council, it was said, was reluctant to make these demolition orders as owners would lose financially, but the government was pressing for rapid slum clearance.

For the owners, Mr. Lewis suggested that a quote of £180 by Robbins (a builder from Weston under Penyard) would renovate No. 27 Edde Cross Street which they could then rent out at 10s. or 12s. per week. Mr. Brown wished to convert Nos. 28 and 29 Edde Cross Street into one house and wanted to renovate Nos. 30 and 31, but withdrew objections to the demolition of Nos. 32 and 33. Dr. Cam opposed the demolition order on Nos. 27 and 28 Alton Street as they were part of his own old Tudor house and properly renovated they would be suitable for an elderly couple rather than a family; in due course an unknown figure was agreed for their renovation. Mr. Bird protested that he could renovate No. 5 Greytree Road for £120. Mr. Aure proposed spending £320 on renovation work on Nos. 3 and 5 Greytree Road and asked if the Council could modify their requirements to hasten his work. He was firmly told that this was not an option as his properties had first been inspected in 1919 and demolition was proposed at that time. A.J. Dean informed the Council that he could not demolish his six cottages in Kyrle Street for fear of damaging Council property, but this was not accepted by the Council who gave him a deadline to complete the demolition or they would do it themselves. Lock objected on the grounds of hardship as it was his own home he would have to demolish! The owner of Nos. 20 and 21 Edde Cross Street said that these were semi-detached properties that could be renovated. Mr. Clift said he planned to knock down two cottages at the back of his houses in Overross Street to improve the others. Mr. Symonds, a builder, quoted £250–£300 to renovate Nos. 13 and 14 Alton Street as they were in a good area and not overcrowded. This latter proposal must have been accepted as these houses are still standing, but all the others, save 23–25 Brampton Street, were confirmed for clearance.

Standing on the corner of Brookfield Road these three cottages were the subject of the only appeal that was upheld against the Council's demolition orders. Their owners had vigorously opposed the Council's efforts to include them in the clearance orders and regarded their property, bought in 1927 for £200, as an investment, providing a large part of their income. On 24 January 1935 Ellen and Lucy Gemmidge duly appealed against the decision by Ross on Wye Urban District Council to demolish Nos. 23, 24 & 25 Brampton Street. The appeal was heard by Judge J.R. Kennedy at Ross County Court and although the list of defects was long and the owners' estimates for repair work to bring them up to a habitable standard varied between £230 and £260, against the Council's estimate of £397, he quashed the demolition orders. The sisters then had to carry out the repairs within a three month period to a revised estimate of £275 and to the Council's satisfaction. This appeal cost the Council £73 in legal fees which they noted, rather peevishly,

The report on 49–51 Edde Cross Street on 11 April 1935 stated that the ceilings were only 6ft. to 7ft. 3ins. high, that windows fell short of the desired size, that there were no larders, no sinks and no sculleries. Separate wash houses were in deplorable condition, the WC was defective and cisterns were in a state of disrepair. The average distance from a house to a WC was 36 feet. There was damp everywhere with defective floors, walls, ceilings and dangerously steep stairs in one house with no handrails. 'Closure' was recommended.

Beside these houses the ruins of a partially demolished house show what parts of Ross looked like at that time. These houses, beside the Pheasant Inn, eventually became the location for the St. John's Ambulance Brigade headquarters.

'would have to be born by the ratepayers in the next financial year'. Now renumbered, the houses still stand on the corner of Brookfield Street overlooking what is now a very different residential area.

Following on from this inquiry, the Council published the following notice in the *Ross Gazette* on 27 June 1935:

Housing Acts 1925 and 1930
Edde Cross Street No. 1 Clearance Order 1935 notice is hereby given that Ross-on-Wye Urban District Council under the powers invested in them by the Housing Act 1930 on 24 June 1935 made a Clearance Order which will be submitted to the Ministry of Health ordering the demolition of the buildings described in the schedule and their vacation within the period specified.
No. 6, 7, 9, 10, 12, 13, 20, 21, Edde Cross Street and their outbuildings and appurtenances used in connection therewith.

Similar Clearance Orders were published at the same time for nos. 49, 50, 51 Edde Cross Street; for 5 Greytree and 1–5, the Nursery; for 29–34 Kyrle Street; for 14–21 Morley Square; and for 27–33 Edde Cross Street. Further orders were issued on 29 July 1935 for 1–10 Broadmead Terrace and 11–13 Station Street; for 1–7 The Folley, Overross; for 24–27 Overross Street and, separately, for 31–37 Overross Street and 25–30 Wolverhampton Terrace, Millpond Street.

On 29 December 1935 the Council recommended that the sum of £10 be expended for taking photographs in connection with the clearance areas. George W. Young secured the commission, and although he initially submitted a bill for £16 4s. he finally settled on £12 16s. 6d., which was paid on 21 January 1936. Sixty years later these photographs are recognised as important historical documents showing long forgotten parts of Ross on Wye and as such are now priceless.

Having said nothing about the long overdue and fundamental improvements the Council was making to social conditions in Ross on Wye, the Chamber of Commerce was quick to complain about the ugly demolition sites that appeared, comparing them to the bombarded and ruined villages in France during the First World War. The Chamber of Commerce also petitioned the Council about the dangerous condition of Cross House (the scene of a bad fire) and various eyesores in Brampton and Overross Streets which, they claimed, were affecting the tourist trade. In response the Council reiterated its policy and claimed that the word demolition had not been defined in law, for the sites were not being flattened in the same way that we now attribute to 'demolition'. It was the Council's policy to simply make condemned houses uninhabitable by insisting that owners removed roofs and gutted the interiors. In some cases walls had to be left standing to support adjoining inhabited houses. If site owners did not utilise their sites within 18 months the Council had powers to take them over compulsorily at valuation, but the owners requested inflated prices above those which the District Auditor would have sanctioned. In some ways this suited the Council as it was cheaper to develop greenfield sites. Even so, some suitable cleared sites were purchased at a rate of £240 an acre. For example Mr. Locke sold the site of 9–13 Edde Cross Street to the Council. As rebuilding during the Second World War was impossible they turned it into a temporary car park for the duration of the war at a cost of £8 for alterations to the pavement. It was only in the 1960s that new flats, houses and light industrial factories were built in Brampton Street, an area that hundreds of people were glad to turn their backs on. Understandably it is an area where no photographic records seem to exist. In the meantime the Council had no authority under the Housing Acts to compel owners to clear their sites of rubble from the demolitions. Neither could they clear it themselves unless it was a nuisance under the Public Health Acts — mere unsightliness did not constitute a nuisance.

Thus extensive eyesores began to develop and were remarked upon by a number of visitors to Ross, as indicated by several letters in the *Ross Gazette*, such as the one on page 62 published on 16 September 1937:

How ideas of house design have changed over the years! The present neat modern houses in Morley Square could not be more different from these old terraced cottages. They were built by the Ross Gas Company about 1830 and at that time were the best in working class housing. Their entrance to New Street was through a 38ft. long passage just 3ft. 8ins. wide beside a cottage now demolished to provide the current vehicular access. A report of 29 March 1935 noted: 'Cobblestones down the centre to divide property on either side. ... At lower end stand wash houses and WC. There was also a WC at South West for women and children who occupy three cottages, while at the lower end there is a WC and urinal for men only and one WC for women and one for children provided for occupants of other five cottages. Maximum distance from cottages 70ft., minimum 37ft. No. 15 has two rooms on ground floor and two bedrooms. No. 16 is an extremely damp cottage with living room, parlour, two bedrooms plus a separate wash house. The other six have just a living room, larder, coal store and two bedrooms. No drains. No inside water supply. No sculleries. Only one exit except one cottage. No through ventilation as all the windows are on the front of the cottages. Ceilings are only 7ft. 3ins. high. Pantile roofs, crumbling mortar, decayed walls, chimney stacks and spouting defective. No gardens, just a narrow strip of land behind 24, 25 New Street for drying clothes. All have damp defective walls, defective floors and ceilings, chimneys and guttering, quite inadequate drainage. Woodwork bad on floors, doors, windows and stairs'. A sub-committee of the Housing Committee inspected the site in April 1935 and recommended demolition. The present smart, modern houses were built in the 1960s.

Trenchard Street, the lower part of Edde Cross Street below Kyrle Street, contained many old, worn-out houses some originally built on the north side of the street for farm workers and other poor labourers. J.E. Haine, the Medical Officer of Health, reported on 14 December 1933 that three adults lived at No. 27, where the floors were bad, walls damp, and repairs were needed to the stairs, that the upstairs ceilings were fallen, the cupboard ceiling 'gone, open to the sky, roof above very defective' (unsurprisingly!), that the back bedroom was ruinous, a back door was needed, the wash house ruinous, a lavatory in the garden had no flush, and the drains poor. Mr. Russell was the tenant.

Mrs. Roden was the tenant of No. 28 where three people lived. Here there was no through ventilation, the woodwork was gone, the walls very damp and crumbling, ceilings coming down and the flagged floors very broken. There was no wash house, and the lavatory was out of order — although shared by two homes. The stairs were described as bad and dangerous. Upstairs the ceilings were boarded so as to keep them up, the walls crumbling and the floors bad. All the woodwork was reported as rotten and in need of replacing.

A Closing Order had already been served on No. 29, but had never been carried out. Mr. and Mrs. Brooke and their three children lived in this dreadful house at a weekly rent of 10s. The walls were rotten and crumbling, with no ventilation, bad woodwork, broken floors and no cooking stove. The walls upstairs were very wet, the windows did not open, the ceilings were boarded up and the wash house was ruinous. The tap and lavatory was shared with No. 28 and the report declared that the houses should be treated as back to back. Demolition was the only solution.

The sites of these cottages now provide access to the houses overlooking the Rope Walk.

Cross House was on the corner between Brampton Street and Over Ross Street, facing the five-ways junction. In 1867 William Williams was a confectioner, grocer and baker at Cross House, Brookend, as seen on this 1912 post-card overlooking children playing in the road junction. By 1909 he was also sub-postmaster at Brookend Post Office which he had installed in his well-stocked stores. After his death his daughters ran a slowly failing business and used part of the large building as a boarding house. By 1935 the Medical Officer of Health's report on housing considered for demolition read:

> 1, 2, 3 Over Ross Street. This building was previously used as a common lodging house, and owing to its closure was converted into three dwellings. The ground floor room (kitchen) of No. 1 is occupied by Miss Williams in conjunction with her shop facing the Millpond, the first and second floor being occupied by Mr. H. Rowberry. The air space at the rear is very limited, and the general structural conditions leave much to be desired. Assuming that the shop, these three cottages and the garage in Brampton Street, were pulled down, a good open space would be available near the railway bridge, and would effect a considerable improvement. Suggest purchase of site and erection of a lavatory.

Cross House suffered a disastrous fire later in 1935 and was bought by Ross U.D.C. in March 1940 for a street widening scheme needed by the increasing volume of traffic on this narrow junction. Cross House and the cottages beyond were demolished immediately and despite wartime shortages the junction was enlarged to its present proportions. A public convenience was subsequently built here in the 1950s, only to be replaced in 1988 by a display of Ross railway history. On the left of Cross House and past the railway viaduct are a few of the 50 cottages in Brampton Street. When the railway was built in 1855, the roadway in Brampton Street was lowered underneath the viaduct to give carts enough headroom, resulting in pavements some 3 feet above the road.

Opposite page: On 11 April 1935 a report on slum properties in Overross Street noted that No. 31 was tenanted by Mr. Paxton and three other adults in a house needing only minor repairs but that it had very poor ventilation and small windows. For Nos. 32–35 it noted that all four properties wanted repairs to floors, roofs, walls and drains. The six houses used one tap for water and though each had a lavatory, none flushed and no water was laid on.

Mr. Counsell was the tenant of No. 36, which was inhabited by three children and four adults. It was recommended for demolition as it was dark and damp, and had no through ventilation. Mr. Stevens dwelt at No. 37 with two other adults and three children. It was a house of three stories, dark and badly ventilated. Demolition or reconstruction by joining into No. 36 was recommended.

This area is now a car park; the last houses here being demolished in the early 1970s when the last tenant moved out. The white house on the end of the row is the Plough Inn.

This page: Beyond the Plough Inn was Griffith's Overross Garage which later expanded across the site of these houses into the premises known today. A detailed report on 13 June 1935 reported that No. 27 had a small living room and parlour approached by a passageway. The bedrooms were the worst feature with badly planned low ceilings and poor ventilation. No. 26 was similar but had a very dark small living room 174 feet square. Of Nos. 24 and 25 the report stated: 'The floor area consists of a small living room and a dark back lobby, one front bedroom, the stairs leading to a landing bedroom. The floor area was 390 square feet, the window area was deficient. As there was no pantry or scullery accommodation most work must be done in the living room. Outside was a poor wash house in a small enclosed yard 159 yards square. Fifteen people lived in these four houses, one containing seven'. All were to be condemned and Clearance Orders were submitted to the Ministry of Health on 24 June 1935.

Sir,

Ross-on-Wye! What picture does the name conjure before your eyes! I imagined a lovely town nestling on the banks of the river amidst the beautiful scenery of the Wye Valley but what a disappointment awaited me. I found hovels half fallen down or partly pulled down and left; dirty little houses with windows smashed; also two or three places where I suppose the people of Ross dump all their old cars, bedsteads and such lumber. Having a young baby in a perambulator the river to me was inaccessible, my way being barred by countless cattle gates. There is one point upon which I can congratulate your Council, and that is, there is no charge made to visit the ruins of Brampton Street. Your surrounding scenery is wonderful but Ross leaves much to be desired.

Yours faithfully,

E.W. Brown, Stanmore, Middx.

Meanwhile some of the Council's earlier housing efforts had to be brought up to date in the 1930s, replacing the defective cooking stoves at Redhill and installing electricity in the four Millpond Street houses.

On 28 May 1936 the Urban District Council agreed to purchase 20 acres of land at Three Crosses for £1,200 to be used for a further 80 houses that were needed to cope with the demand created by the Houses (Overcrowding) Act 1935. Intended to attack the gross overcrowding in inner city slums, it could also be used in towns like Ross where the situation was endemic. Workers' wages were so low in Ross and other towns that sub-letting was one of the few ways to increase family income; as a result of the Act this became illegal if it led to overcrowding. Councils were empowered to control numbers by listing the permitted inhabitants in the rent book.

Administrative delays in the Three Crosses building contract and the failure of the architect to draw up plans in good time resulted in a rush for the contractor, Wilesmith and Son, to complete the houses by 31 December 1938 when the subsidy scheme under which they were built came to an end. In the event, the contract was officially completed and the tenants given their keys on New Year's Eve, much to everyone's relief. Of the 80 planned houses 56 were actually built. The eight four-bedroomed houses rented at 8s. 6d., eight two-bedroomed at 6s. 6d., and the 40 three-bedroomed at 7s. 6d. together alleviated the worst of Ross's overcrowding problems. Such was the state of affairs that the goods of 14 tenants from the bug-infested properties they vacated had to be fumigated before they moved into their new homes!

However, this new development and associated demolitions was not the end of all the bad housing in Ross. When a local draper asked a visiting sales representative 'Can I order 24 loose ladies handker-chiefs?', she gained the response 'Are there that number of loose women in Ross?' Certainly, for a time during the Second World War, one area that is now demolished had a certain reputation for prostitution, where large numbers of servicemen and poor social conditions contributed to such behaviour. Wartime shortages prevented further building until 1950 when conditions became easier for the final phases of the social rehousing, associated with the clearances of slums, that for too long had been a blot on Ross on Wye.

Standing out from all the other Council officers, the man most responsible for the town's slum clear-ance, Mr. Frank Ricketts, the Sanitary Inspector, retired in October 1938 after 47 years' work in the town. Twenty years after his first report stated that Ross needed 169 new houses he could see 192 had been built and, thanks to his endeavours, the worst of the slum houses had been finally swept away.

Detailed records of when the houses were demolished do not exist as they were all privately owned. Some idea of the size of the rehousing problems that had faced the Ross on Wye Urban District Council can be seen by the fact that as late as the 1974 Local Government reorganisation, the successor South Herefordshire District Council took over 22 houses (in the Nursery Road area) that were scheduled for demolition. In the 50 years between 1920 and 1970 Ross on Wye Urban District Council had built 574 houses and flats, 192 before 1940 and 382 after the war and deserve much credit for the way they tackled the serious problems caused by bad housing and the associated social effects.

By 1955 the land behind the demolished cottages in Brampton Street had become very overgrown with weeds and brambles, and provided a great playground for local chidren. Even in Brampton Street parents warned their children not to play with children from certain homes or not to play in some areas. Margaret Allen ignored these warnings one day and while playing spinning on some railings bumped her head badly. Occasional aches still remind her of her mother's warning 50 years later!

The Game Cock Inn was situated 30 yards. above the railway viaduct on the west side of Brampton Street. After the occupants of the condemned houses moved out to the new estates, the pub lost many of its regular customers and trade slowly drifted away. It closed in 1958 and was sold to a builder in 1960 as a private house. He demolished it a few years later as part of a building development.

Top left: Mr. and Mrs. Bridges lived at 43 Overross Street for 47 years from 1905 to 1952.

Top right: This 1955 photograph shows a happy well-dressed family group and their Saturday shopping on a flat cart outside the back of the Game Cock Inn. Linda Allen and her older sister Margaret sit between their cousins Nigel and Martin Waldron and their grandfather George Webb, a long-serving 'saw doctor' at Kemp's saw mill.

Bottom left: The publican's wife, Dorothy Allen, poses with Toby Marshall, one of their old customers, outside the Game Cock in 1952.

Bottom right: Linda Allen plays with her pet dog on the well-worn steps that used to lead from the raised pavement to the road.

Chapel Lamps
Hentland
Nr Ross

june 4   19

Sir

I am sending you 10 shillings on account of rent I have asked Mr Hall to come and do the repairs but he have not been I should be glad if you would write to him about it for the wet have come in the bedrooms auful me and the children have had to stay downstair of a night owing to the wet comeing in the rooms

I am your truly

N. Gwilliam

Above: Despite their difficult circumstances, people tried to make the best of their talents. Mr Pullen's advertisement appeared in a 1924 programme for the Kyrle Picture Palace. Mr. Pullen was one of several shoe repairers in the town in an age when people wore out their shoes and had them repaired rather than throwing them away as we do today.

Left: Although Mr. Gwilliam wrote this desperate letter to his unsympathetic landlord from Hentland, it is quite obvious from the Sanitary Inspector's reports that many similar complaining letters were ignored by local slum landlords whose urge to make money overcame any social scruples of fairness or decency for their unfortunate tenants.

Below: This photograph, from the corner of Millpond Street and Station Street, shows the enormous changes in this small area of Ross on Wye in the last 60 years. After Wolverhampton and Broadmead Terraces had been demolished the site became part of Kemp's timber yard. Safeways (now Morrisons) used this part of their site for a petrol forecourt and car park. Kemp's had built the large warehouse after a serious fire in 1975. The white building in the right distance was the communal school kitchen erected in the 1940s to supply school dinners to all the schools in the area.

CHAPTER FIVE

The Workhouse, Cottage Hospital and St. John's Ambulance Brigade

The Workhouse

The first Poor Laws were introduced in the reign of Henry VIII with further legislation in 1601. However, the economic depression that followed the Napoleonic wars and the increase in population led to the Poor Law Amendment Act of 1834. This gave local unions of parishes, who were responsible for their poor, powers to build workhouses for their destitute inhabitants and to administer out-relief to the poor who were no longer able to look after themselves.

Mr. Evans chaired the first meeting of the Ross Board of Guardians at the Swan Inn on 5 May 1836, where it was resolved to build a new workhouse to replace the existing ones at Weston, Upton Bishop and Ross. The weekly meeting then moved to Walter Scott's schoolroom in the summer. The site for the workhouse in Alton Street was bought for £500 and an architect, Mr. Plowman, was engaged to draw up plans for £50. On 4 August 1836 the Board of Guardians accepted a tender of £2,200 from Thomas Trisham of Ross to be ready by August the following year. However, he tried to cut corners with substandard workmanship and fittings, meaning that it was not ready for occupation until early 1838, under Mr. Jeffreys as the first master. The Board held its first fortnightly meeting in their new boardroom on 16 November 1837 where they were concerned with the administration of out-relief to the poor of the 30 parishes in Herefordshire, together with Ruardean in Gloucestershire, that comprised the Union, an area that contained a population of about 16,000.

Built to accommodate a staff of nine and 200 inmates, the workhouse continued in use for many years with major alterations in 1872. This included a new wing for tramps, who being homeless, could only be offered temporary accommodation. The average number of inmates was about 100 with a varying (and perhaps decreasing) number of tramps, especially when compulsory baths were introduced! In two weeks in March 1901, 31 men, 7 women and 11 children were given overnight accommodation in return for some light tasks. To pay for their stay the men had to break five hundredweight of roadstone before leaving the next morning. Failure to do their allotted task meant 14 days in prison, which was an option some tramps took in winter time. The 1914 Poor Law Reform Act gave local Guardians more control in running their workhouses. Better trained staff were to be employed and proper records kept. Married couples over 60 were given their own accommodation and no child could be an inmate for more than six weeks.

Staff and inmates grew some of their own vegetables in the gardens and on the Royal Cross Estate opposite and ran a small farm with pigs and other stock. As well as income from the rates, extra funds were obtained by the sale of livestock, firewood and roadstone.

Some idea of the finances are given by the 1913 accounts, which show an income of £9,172 and expenditure of £8,175. The introduction of the old age pension in 1911 cut the amount of out-relief considerably, but the Ross Guardians topped up the pension of 5s. by up to 4s. 6d. extra and gave 1s. each week as winter relief.

No. 6956   **HEREFORDSHIRE COUNTY COUNCIL.**   Receipt.

2?ᵗʰ day of _February_ 193?

Received of _Mr Pascoe_

the sum of _Five Shillings_   5/-

in respect of _____ Cwt. of Firewood _100_ Bundles of Wood.

(Signed) _____

_____ Master.

Ross   **Poor Law Institution.**

Top: This enlargement of an aerial photograph taken about 1930 gives some idea of the size of the Union Workhouse buildings. Large gardens in the front supplied the inmates with vegetables. In 1995 it was demolished and the Community Hospital and Alton Street Surgery were built on the site. Cars are now parked on the old gardens. Like the slums, the workhouse was hardly ever photographed although it was close to the town centre and over 100 people lived there. It must have been that the potential sales would have been too low to make postcards worthwhile

Above: A receipt from the Poor Law Institution for 5s. for supplying 100 bundles of wood to Mr. Pascoe in 1934.

Left: A letter accompanying a cheque for £361 8s. 9d. being the payment for the county and police rates on the Ross Union Workhouse in 1857.

These terms were more generous and humane than other places in the county and certainly the grim conditions in some workhouses were not repeated in Ross. Local people also provided various comforts, especially at Christmas, and all sorts of unexpected extras. In 1913, for example, inmates were given free entry to the Kyrle Picture Palace matinées and the following year had free admission to a travelling theatre at Smallbrook Gardens. In 1930 Mrs. Moffat hosted an afternoon tea for 80, with flowers, sweets and presents for everybody. June 1932 saw an outing to Barry Island costing £28 12s. 6d. funded by a number of whist drives. Reading the fortnightly accounts of the Board's meetings the impression is that the workhouse was run as humanely as possible.

The last meeting of the Board of Guardians was held on 20 March 1930, its powers being taken over on 1 April by Herefordshire County Council under the Local Government Act.

The Cottage Hospital

The Dispensary and Cottage Hospital in Gloucester Road was built in 1879 at a cost of £1,200 raised by local public subscription. It had ten beds, two cots for children and a ward for private cases. An operating theatre was added in 1897 and in 1921 an annex to the old wards was erected together with a special ward for children. These additions and an X-Ray room cost another £3,000.

To cover its running costs the hospital charged people who could afford treatment, but for most of its day to day expenditure it depended on continual fundraising events and the perennial generosity of the local population and their organisations. Many better-off families paid an annual subscription. Every week the *Ross Gazette* published a list of donors, sometimes anonymous. Well-wishers even donated vegetables, fruit, salmon, rhubarb, eggs, apples and other seasonal produce, weekly magazines, tablecloths and an invalid chair.

One spectacular fundraising event that failed was the hospital's air pageant organised annually in the 1930s. One was widely advertised for 4 June 1934 at the Old Race Course (Hildersley) stating that six different aeroplanes, including an airliner, were scheduled to appear. In the event it was poorly attended and raised

The Ross Cottage Hospital had a life of nearly 120 years, being built in 1879 and demolished in 1997.

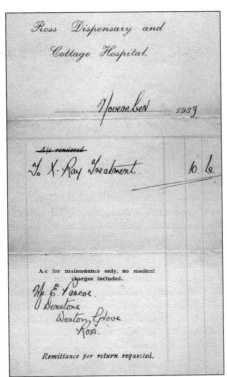

Ross Dispensary and Cottage Hospital.

November 1933

A/c rendered
To X-Ray Treatment.   10. 6

A/c for maintenance only, no medical
charges included.

Mr. E. Pascoe.
Denstone
Weston Grove
Ross.

Remittance per return requested.

a mere £10. In 1932 over 3,000 people bought shilling raffle tickets for an Austin Seven car, so raising over £150.

Even capital works had to be funded locally. There was no National Health Service to provide the money needed for building improvements and extensions. In October 1934 the Management Committee appealed for another £600 to provide an isolation ward, improvements to the men's lavatories and a recreation room for the nursing staff. £225 had already been raised by local subscriptions and an urgent request was made for the remainder. The appeal finally reached £696 11s. 6d., but was not quite enough to cover the builder's bill from Messrs. Bettington of £719. These much-needed improvements were recognised as leading to more efficient running of the hospital. Local wealthy benefactors, such as Mrs. Foster of Brockhampton Court, frequently made up deficiencies and donated generously to appeals.

The 1935 hospital report gives some idea how much it was used. It treated 219 in-patients (218 in 1934) 839 out-patients (1,147 in 1934) and carried out 103 operations (120 in 1934). 10 to 15 beds were occupied daily costing £2 19s. per week. There were 95 X-ray treatments (120 in 1934). Expenditure was £1,767 8s. 7d. and income £1,726. There was £65 15s. owing from some patients for their treatments. Management was then carried out at a very local level, unlike much of the present day Health Service management.

This much-loved Cottage Hospital was demolished in 1997 and the site has since been redeveloped as retirement flats.

St. John's Ambulance Brigade

After a lapse of many years the Ross St. John's Ambulance Brigade was reformed on Wednesday 18 March 1931 at a meeting at the New Theatre. Thirty men enrolled at 5s. annual subscription. The aim was to train sufficient men to a high enough standard to crew an ambulance. There was an urgent need for such a service in the area because of the large number of traffic accidents, when the injured were often conveyed to hospital in the first car, lorry or bus willing to make the journey. At that time the nearest ambulance was stationed at Monmouth. Dr. Haine offered to teach the recruits First Aid; Major Butcher of the T.A. offered the Drill Hall as a venue for the classes; and G. Eltome and T.C. Sherwood were elected joint secretaries.

By 1934 there was a training brigade, comprising one superintendent, one sergeant, three corporals and 25 privates. Mr. Wheeler was in charge of the newly-formed Youth Cadet Corps whose 36 youngsters were described as 'very keen'. But there was already an urgent need for a new motor ambulance to replace the aged Morris that had been their transport since they started. The Brigade ran a series of fund raising events and canvassed local organisations for support for the £600 needed for a new machine. Eventually a new Austin 20

ambulance was purchased in April 1934 and dedicated at a service at the Market House on Sunday 6 May. The Revd. E.H. Beattie officiated with other religious denominations assisting, and music was provided by the Town Band conducted by Ivan Constance. For this important occasion the Brigade paraded in full dress uniform including water bottles and service medals, with S. Nemo, the transport secretary, and T.C. Sherwood, by then treasurer, driving the new vehicle. The next week the ambulance was in action taking a lady from Symonds Yat, where she had broken her ankle, to Gloucester Hospital.

The 1934 annual report of the Ross on Wye St. John's Ambulance Brigade noted that its members had provided 913 hours of road patrols and 756 hours of public services. The ambulance had attended 31 accidents, provided transport in 80 other cases and had been driven over 1,500 miles. The ambulance was kept at Passey & Son's garage in Gloucester Road and Mr. Lerego, owner of the Castle Garage, provided 4 gallons of free petrol every month. The only expense was 8s. 6d. for a new door handle 'as the hospital entrance was extremely narrow'! The 1935 report contained thanks to the Governors of Ross Cottage Hospital for widening the gateway thus 'Making the work easier for the ambulance drivers'.

In 1937 they acquired three slum clearance sites in Edde Cross Street as a place far their much-needed new garage and headquarters, and having raised £876 of the £1,000 necessary by April 1938, were able to start their building.

Top: The new ambulance, purchased in 1934, outside the Chase Hotel.

Middle: This 1943 photograph of Ross on Wye St. John's Ambulance Nursing Section includes Gussie and Marjorie Preedy, Nellie Smith, Hazel Watkins, Doreen and Phyllis Brown.

Bottom: A 1933 photograph of the St. John Ambulance Brigade displaying their trophies. From the left: Sgt. George Eltome, Alan Nemo, unknown, Frank James. (Photo courtesy of Mr. Nemo)

CHAPTER SIX

Roads and Railways

Before the establishment of toll roads in the 18th century, communications and trade were slow and expensive because of the poor condition of the roads. To help improve travel conditions locally the Ross Turnpike Trust was set up in 1749 and soon 11 routes totalling 43 miles radiated from Ross to Gloucester, Harewood End, Hoarwithy, How Caple and Much Marcle. Further Acts in 1773, 1791, 1815, and 1862 extended the network further. A scheme for a new road to the furnaces at Bishopswood, including the Kerne Bridge crossing of the Wye to Goodrich village, replacing the ford below Goodrich castle, was one such addition in the 1820s. Improved communications along the new toll roads allowed manufactured goods to be transported more easily than in previous centuries. Even so, transport was slow and costly until the advent of the railways really opened rural Herefordshire for trade with the rest of England and beyond.

Coaching, apart from some running into Wales and summer tourist trips, ceased in Ross in 1873 when the Ross and Monmouth railway was opened. The railways provided large scale employment at a time when every possible care was taken to give service to their passengers and customers.

As the century progressed other industries developed in Ross. The gas works in Kyrle Street provided both employment and houses for their workers in Morley Square and Kyrle Street. The Kell brothers developed an agricultural machinery works by the mill pond, and Kemp's timber yard opened in Henry Street. Perkins and Bellamy ran an iron foundry in the Crofts

The arrival of the railway in 1855 led to an immediate loss of trade in the coaching industry. The old coaching inns of Ross suffered heavy financial losses until they managed to re-organise. Horse-drawn coaches continued to run into Wales after the railway reached Monmouth in 1873. After this date sightseeing tourist coaches operated only during the season. This is one of the last mail coaches in Ross. It was owned by Pryce Hamilton of Wilton House and ran daily from Ross to Chepstow before the arrival of the railways. Like the other vehicles operating from the Royal Hotel this was painted pale yellow.

Top: Timber and wood products have always been an important part of the county's economy, with sawmills serving the more heavily wooded areas. Here William Price of Walford stands in Gloucester Road beside his 1913 Garrett traction engine No. 31118 (Reg. No: BJ 1570) ready to tow a huge oak trunk to be sawn into planks, probably at Kemp's timber yard in Millpond Street.

Left: In 1915 Alley & MacLellan moved their business from Glasgow to larger premises in Shrewsbury. Their Sentinel Waggon Works continued making steam lorries there until 1938. Even as late as 1950 they supplied 100 steam-powered waggons to the Argentine.

There were two types of steam waggon. The overtype owed its design to the traction engine where the mechanical works were above the boiler, whilst the undertype had an enclosed mechanism beneath the boiler.

Sentinels seem to have photographed each new waggon in the owner's livery at their works before delivery. This was Sentinel's Standard 6 ton undertype waggon in production from 1906 to the late 1920s. Sturdy and robust it delivered stock feed, seeds and fertilizers in the Ross area for the South Herefordshire Agricultural Co-operative Society. Even in 1922 it was limited to a 12 mph speed limit, although this was probably a comfortable speed for a lorry with an open cab on solid tyres and acetylene lamps running on the primitive roads of rural Herefordshire.

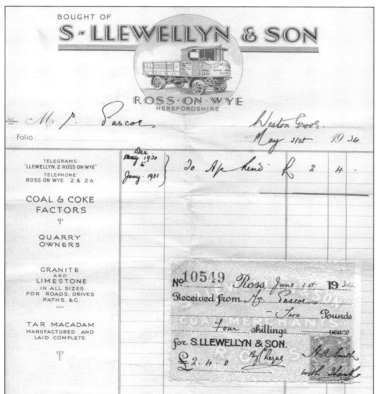

Above: Llewellyn & Son bought this 10-ton Sentinel S6 steam lorry about 1933 for stone and coal deliveries in the area. It was still subject to a 20 mph speed limit. By this time steam lorries had copied the appearance of their petrol counterparts with inflated rubber tyres, enclosed cab, mirrors and electric headlamps (powered by a dynamo and batteries). Robust and economical in their time this type of steam wagon continued in use for 20 years, eventually being superceded by the more efficient and faster diesel lorries.

Left: Llewellyn and Son must have been long suffering at the hands of Mr. Pascoe who finally paid his account of 1930–31 in June 1936. The reminder is duly stamped as a receipt.

George and William Butcher renamed their bicycle shop The Motor House and rebuilt it as a car showroom as cars became more popular in the first decade of the 20th century and the internal combustion engine took over from horse and pedal power. They pose with their staff outside their showroom in Brookend Street for this advertisement photograph.

The gates on the right led to Ross Electric Light and Power Company's generating works. In 1902 they laid on a power supply round the town, trying to undercut the Ross Gas Company's prices under the guidance of their engineer, secretary and manager Mr. Talford Ely. In 1914 he installed a new Hindley vertical suction gas engine to improve performance and efficiency, proudly inviting anyone interested in electricity or engineering to inspect the new generator in 'the brick building just inside the gates anytime during working hours'. The company was later taken over by the Shropshire, Worcestershire and Staffordshire Electric Supply Company whose supply covered the whole area.

Their gateway is now the entrance to the garage workshop, so that cars no longer have to use the doorway on the corner of the building.

where the Alpha Fire Extinguishing Company also had their works. These were absorbed into the Blake empire in 1895 and 1910. The country's economy grew with the expansion of the railway network. The industries in the Ross area benefited like everywhere else from their arrival. They brought raw materials and fuel and distributed finished goods around the country, propelling Ross into the modern age. The railways were a long-term investment which should have been modernised and not dismantled.

Two years after reaching Hereford from Shrewsbury, a railway line was built to Gloucester and was opened to Ross in June 1855 at last providing an efficient transport system both to the midlands markets and eventually to the rest of the country. As a typical Great Western Railway Station, its plans were used in building the new station at Kidderminster on the restored Severn Valley Railway.

The picturesque line to Monmouth opened in August 1873, but the subsequent increased competition from cars, buses and lorries led to its closure on 4 January 1959. With hindsight this was a great pity as a steam passenger service down the Wye valley to Chepstow would have attracted thousands of extra tourists to the area each year.

Top: Ross station as seen by the camera of R.E. Davies in 1906 with a train about to set off for Hereford. At the end of the goods bay on the left are two hinged ramps to enable wagons and other wheeled vehicles to be loaded onto flat trucks. In 1911 in its heyday the GWR employed 37 men at Ross plus R.T. Smith's contract hauliers. As a tribute to them for not taking part in the nationwide railwaymen's strike in August, when the Army was used to keep order in several towns, local businessmen subscribed over £43, giving each railwayman a guinea and others 10s. 9d. for their loyalty to the community against their union workmates.

Right: A note on the reverse of this postcard says it is the 10.20 am passenger train from Hereford to Gloucester ready to leave Ross on 16 April 1935. For the convenience of passengers, and to save them from having to change trains at Gloucester, through carriages were available which connected with the Gloucester train to Paddington.

Bottom right: The train from Monmouth, drawn by a 0-4-2 tank engine No. 4820, has just arrived in the bay at Ross station. The guard's van door stands open for the parcels and packets to be unloaded while the driver patiently waits. The railway companies operated an efficient nationwide delivery system for parcels of all sorts long before the modern fleets of white vans raced around our roads.

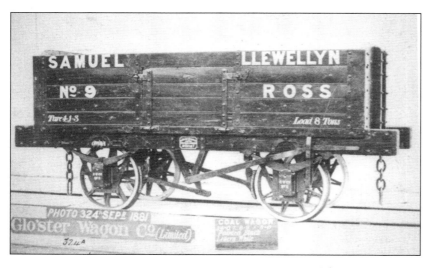

Top: Two young train spotters watch the train from Hereford enter Ross station in August 1960. Details of the track layout, signals' gantry, water tower and goods shed can all be clearly seen.

Centre: The engine shed faced west towards Ross on Wye station as it was situated between the junction of the Gloucester and Monmouth lines. The double tracks in the foreground merged into the single track to Monmouth. In the background a passenger train passes on its way to Gloucester. The best and most imposing of the remaining railway buildings in Ross on Wye, the old engine shed was well built and despite looking out of place among the modern industrial buildings surrounding it, it could easily outlive them all.

Bottom: Gloucester Wagon Company made thousands of coal wagons like this both for the multitude of different railway companies who all depended on coal for fuel, and for the hundreds of private companies who owned their own wagons of various styles to transport their freight. Samuel Llewellyn ran a coal business in the station yard and purchased at least nine wagons before 1881 to carry coal from pits in South Wales and the Forest of Dean. They were of very simple design, without buffers, had only rudimentary hand operated brakes and were hooked together with loose chains. Once arrived at their destination the eight-ton load of coal had to be shovelled out by hand into carts or hundredweight sacks for local sale. No wonder gas and electricity became so universally popular.

Top: Broad Meadows is the large level field behind the station which at times was used for displays and fetes and on this hot day in 1908 was the setting for a carnival. Everyone wore a hat — caps, straw boaters and top hats on the men and mostly large feather-trimmed hats for the ladies, some carried parasols to avoid the hot sun.

The details of the back of the station are noteworthy with the surprisingly high glazed footbridge overlooking the scene. That and the long platform canopy protected the passengers from the elements until they boarded their trains. A rake of goods wagons stands in the loop ready to depart. Beyond the station the chimneys of the houses in North Road are visible above the canopy.

Left: Soon after the arrival of the railway, Station Street was constructed to give better access to the lower part of the town. In 1865 Alton Court Brewery built their brewery and malthouse on each side of the street, brewing beer until 1956, the brewery being demolished in the 1980s. The combined aroma of hops and malting barley sometimes made it 'the sweetest smelling street in Ross'. On the opposite side of the street the timbered premises of Thomas Ryall's builders and funeral furnishing suffered the same fate and now provide a service access to the modern shops in the Maltings arcade. This peaceful scene is in complete contrast to the present day with a busy street full of parked cars and enormous delivery lorries trying to reverse across it into an inadequate service area.

Captain Alfred Bird and four of his 15 firemen pose with a cup they won in a 1910 competition. The group are in front of their gleaming firefighting equipment in the Palace Yard near the Royal Hotel. Eleven years previously Ross Urban and Rural District Councils combined their resources to buy a new double-vertical steamer, an extending escape ladder and an equipment wagon, hence the name board 'Ross United Councils' on the steamer which was immediately christened the *John Kyrle*. More often than not, poor communications meant a fire was out of control before the horse-drawn steamer could arrive at the scene. To allay people's fears and to help raise funds for the brigade, visits to some of the larger houses in the locality were organised, where the machine's capabilities were demonstrated. By our standards turnout times were very slow and became even worse during the last two years of the First World War. There was such an acute shortage of draught horses everywhere — even for pulling a fire engine in an emergency — that in the event of a fire local farmers were requested to send their own team of horses to pull the fire engine to the blaze!

Mr. and Mrs. Harold Crump of 'Tuffley' in Ryefield Road were so pleased with their new Citreon 5CV tourer that they used this photograph as a Christmas card in 1926. Nicknamed the 'Cloverleaf' from its body shape it was a typical French made light car with a reputation for toughness. Manufactured in Paris between 1922 –25 it was powered by a 856cc. engine and sold for about £225, nearly £100 cheaper than the saloon version. With no windscreen wipers it was not really suitable for driving in rainy weather!

CHAPTER SEVEN

Education

The 1870 Education Act slowly resulted in better schools and education for all school-age children. Its effects were felt in Ross in 1873 with the building of the Board Schools in Cantilupe Road at a cost of £6,000 to replace other schools in the town. After the establishment of the County Council in 1889 it became known as the Council School and was enlarged to accommodate 700 pupils although the average attendance in 1910 was about 600.

Probably the most exciting and memorable episode in the Council school's history was the boys' strike in support of their teachers in February 1914. Herefordshire teachers were among the worst paid in the country and in January and February 1914 they started a well-organised strike to win an improved pay scale from the Herefordshire Education Authority under its formidable chairman, Sir James Rankin M.P. The Education Authority tried to find as many teachers as possible from anywhere in the United Kingdom to break the strike

Before starting morning lessons at the Council School in Cantilupe Road some pupils pose in the early morning winter sunshine in Dickie Davies's photograph. Generations of Ross children started their education here for nearly a century before it was demolished in 1969 as structurally unsafe. It is now the site of a modern housing development next to the new library and only two stone pillars and memories remain of the old school.

Top: Plays, concerts and Christmas nativities are always popular with parents and children alike. Here 37 pupils of Ross County Council School pose in costume in the school yard for a photographic memento of their production of *The Magic Fan* in March 1932.

Left: This is a fine photograph by G.W. Young of the teachers of Ross County Primary School in 1935.
Back row left to right: Mrs. Smith, Mrs. Thomas, Mrs. Salmon, Miss Stevens, Mr. Ball, Mr. Turner, Mr. Moore.
Front row: Miss Faster, Mrs. Dorothy Morgan (née Young), Joyce Davies, Mr. Smith (Headmaster), Mr. Williams, Miss Reece, Mrs. Edwards.

and keep their schools open, but only managed to enlist about 20 from as far away as Cornwall and Scotland. They needed many more than this to break the strike as these teachers were very unpopular and children refused to be taught by them in Ledbury and Ross. In Leominster and many villages the schools closed completely.

In Ross on Friday 29 January the infants and girls were told not to attend school the following Monday. The Headmaster, W.G. Edwards, and two temporary teachers then tried to control 212 boys who reluctantly turned up for school on the Monday. However, many other boys marched around the town in support of their striking teachers. Chanting their slogan 'Strike Boys, Strike', they refused to be taught, jumped out of the school windows, daubed their slogan everywhere and pelted the temporary masters and the police with mud and books. On Tuesday afternoon similar scenes occurred, with boys throwing clods and stones at the police who had been called to restore order. This was followed by another march around the town. There were similar revolutionary scenes at Ledbury Girls School where the girls barricaded the doors and booed the strike-breaking mistresses away.

Worried by the boys' unruly behaviour, Mr. F.S. Collins, the Chairman of the Governors, whose authority had been taken away by the Education Committee's strike-breaking actions, offered the boys 3d. a week each if they would go back to school and behave until the end of the strike! This had the desired effect, especially when he also offered the girls an afternoon tea. On 19 February the strike came to an end when the Government Board of Education forced the Herefordshire Education Authority to accept the teachers demands for a pay scale plus increments, even though this was a scale that would seem pitiful to our eyes today.

The realisation that huge amounts of human talent were wasted without proper secondary education slowly became apparent as industrialisation spread across the country in the 19th century and the need for a better educated workforce arose. The 1902 Education Act enabled towns like Ross to build suitable schools to tap local children's potential. After several years in the planning Sir James Rankin M.P. laid the foundation stone of Ross Secondary School on 8 May 1911 using a special presentation silver trowel and ebony mallet.

A 1911 cartoon by A.M.I. labelled 'Not by the Daily Mirror'.

The cartoon shows Sir James Rankin with his mallet about to lay the foundation stone for the Ross Secondary School. The note attached to the trowel reads 'For Ranky from Small Arthur'.

It is not obvious why the foundation stone, which includes the builder's name — W. Powell and Sons of Hereford — is followed by 'P.A.S. I don't think'.

Unfortunately the political point of the cartoon is rather lost on us now.

A crowd of interested Ross citizens and dignitaries watch as Sir James Rankin, the chairman of Herefordshire County Council's Education Committee, lays the foundation stone of Ross Secondary School on 8 May 1911. This building is now the much-used Larrapeurz Centre.

Sir James returned on Saturday 20 January 1912 to perform the opening ceremony declaring the school 'A benefit and a blessing to the town'. The school opened to its first 41 pupils, 22 of them girls, three days later. Four boys and four girls had won scholarships, but the parents of the rest of the pupils paid £2 5s. per term. There was accommodation for a few boy boarders at the headmaster's house, which was occupied by Arthur Kraest Barker, B.A. formerly of Colchester Royal Grammar School, where he had been senior Maths and Science master. The school was designed to give a higher standard of education than the Council school in Cantilupe Road, but it struggled to attract sufficient students as it was a fee-paying establishment. This was reversed when the 1944 Education Act abolished such fees.

Ross Rural District Council did not support the building of the school which cost the County Council £3,600 and Ross Urban District Council £2,400, thus adding 2d. in the pound to the rates. The annual running costs were recorded as £1,172, including salaries, administration and books. Under their energetic headmaster and his three staff the pupils started fortnightly concerts for families and friends. They also played football matches against the council school and staged a production of Rip Van Winkle at the end of the first term. In the summer term the boys were allowed the use of Ross Cricket Club ground, whilst the girls were lent two tennis courts by the nearby Tennis Club. Later the school was renamed the Grammar School and acquired a 6½-acre playing field at Hildersley for team games.

Top and middle: To promote Ross Secondary School and increase the number of pupils advertisements were regularly placed in local papers.

Henry Palmer, a photographer at 21 Broad Street, was commissioned to produce a series of photographic postcards of the new school to illustrate its large hall, five class rooms, science laboratory, cookery room and workshop.

In the upper photograph eight girls pose in their cookery room equipped with an Eagle range, Eureka gas cooker, larder etc. under the watchful eye of their teacher.

In the middle photograph a mixed group listen to their teacher at the start of a practical lesson in the well-stocked science laboratory.

Bottom: The fee for a term at the Grammar School was four guineas in 1934. Such fees were abolished by the 1944 Education Act.

The bill is receipted with a 2d. postage stamp cancelled by Lloyds Bank's official handstamp. Since Victorian times until relatively recently stamps had to be affixed to all receipts above £1 as a government tax on spending

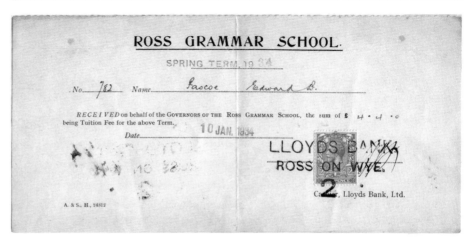

CHAPTER EIGHT

Processions, Sports and Carnivals

Summer weekends in Ross during the first half of the 20th century saw countless processions and carnivals if the numbers of postcards recording these almost forgotten events are anything to judge by. Many were organised as fund-raising events for the Cottage Hospital and other local charities; the popularity of these different parades can be judged by the number of people taking part as well as those just watching. Amateur photographs and postcards are the only visual records of these events for this was before the days when photographs were commonly used in newspapers. To increase their sale potential photographers tried — they could hardly fail — to include as many people as possible, and then published the postcards without captions for everyone knew what was taking place. This makes it difficult some decades later to identify what event was being portrayed with any certainty.

Crowds along Gloucester Road watch a parade of floats and organisations pass by in an effort to raise more money for the Cottage Hospital. Flags and bunting flutter as this 1926 parade passes towards the Market Place. On the left Heins' music shop has its shutters closed against any accidental damage. The two shops behind the banner belonged to South Herefordshire Agricultural Co-operative Society, housing their offices as well as their retail department. In pre-television days the whole town would turn up to see a colourful entertaining parade of this sort and donate generously.

Top left: Members of the King Edward VII Lodge of the Royal Antediluvian Order of Buffaloes in full regalia in 1911.

Lower left: This delightfully casual photograph by Colman Debenham is a souvenir of Ross Cricket Club entertaining E.G. Bibwood's Eleven, a visiting team from Birmingham and North Worcestershire. On 23 and 24 July 1906 they played a two-day match at Ross which the home team narrowly won by a single wicket. One of the visitors sent this postcard as a memento of the event to a young lady living in Brussels.

Colman Debenham had an art shop in Gloucester Road opposite the Post Office. His advertisements stated that he sold picture frames, oil colours, sketch pads and artists' materials. In all his advertisements there was no mention of photography or postcards for which he is now best remembered.

Many workingmen's clubs and societies, some with exotic names, were formed in Victorian and Edwardian times in villages and towns across the country with the aim of helping their members in times of need. With only the Workhouse and Poor Relief to fall back on in times of financial difficulty these movements became very popular and widespread. One such mutual support club in Ross was a branch of the Buffaloes — a nation-wide organization. Named the King Edward VII Lodge of the Royal Antediluvian Order of Buffaloes, it was formed in 1903 both as a mutual help society and to raise money for local charities. The Lodge struggled for the first few years, with only ten members in 1906. However, the bright idea of holding a series of children's teas aroused local awareness and by 1913 membership had risen to 38 and at one of their teas they entertained 1,030 children! They claimed that their strength was due to being a truly workingmen's organisation nation-wide, and that none of their members went without help if in need or distress.

Top right: 'Tilting at the ring' was one of eight different races at the Motor Gymkhana held on the Golf Links on 26 May 1908. Mrs. Capper of Northgate, St. Weonard's is seen here driving her husband's Mayfair. She had done well to spear three rings but history does not record who won the event.

The Mayfair car CJ 48, powered by a 6hp de Dion engine, later belonged to Mr. M.J. Caws of the Valley Hotel who scrapped it in 1921.

Bottom right: Grass track cycle racing provided plenty of entertainment at this Ross carnival sports day sometime in the Edwardian era.

Sporting events included cricket, tennis and golf matches, and even a Motor Gymkhana that was at least held once in 1908. This was advertised as 'the best outdoor attraction of the coming season with plenty of cheap fun and amusement appeal' with races including obstacle, balloon bursting and even a chauffeurs' race. Music was provided by the Cheltenham Rifles Band which entertained the large crowd in the intervals, all well worth the two shillings entrance fee.

In Ross, as elsewhere in the country, cycling was very popular in Edwardian times as a quick and cheap means of travel. Ross Cycle Club organised weekend rides to visit places of interest in the county, often including a picnic. For the more energetic members there were also time trials.

The short-lived Ross Amateur Gymnasium Society was formed in 1903 as an offshoot of the St. Mary's church men's club physical recreation branch. The Society secured a building on the Camp site at Hildersley to practise and raised funds for equipment. They staged annual displays in Ross Corn Exchange, and on 27 March 1906 their performance was accompanied by a string band. Occasionally they also staged popular boxing competitions. The initial enthusiasm eventually faded and by 1912 only a handful of members were attending practices at the Overross Mission Rooms.

To cater for the latest craze of roller skating, both the Corn Exchange and the Rowing Club set up skating rinks in 1910. The Rowing Club's rink was open daily in the winter months charging 6d. per session. The Corn Exchange had three daily sessions at 1s. for men and 9d. for ladies including skates. It even staged rink hockey matches between Hereford, Gloucester and Ross.

Top left: Members of the Ross Amateur Gymnasium Society practicing their routines on Camp Meadow. Their trainer was Ernest James, the athelete in the centre of the tableau. With subscriptions of 3s. 6d. for seniors and 1s. 6d. for boys per session, it was cheap enough for anyone to join. The golf club house is visible in the left distance. The fence shows the line of the Ross to Monmouth railway.

Middle left: Smallbrook Road about 1908 was quiet enough to act as an assembly area for many processions. Although this event cannot be identified, the number of children suggest a Sunday School picnic, whilst the numerous flags indicate it could have been an Empire Day celebration. Whatever the event it was certainly well attended, with everyone dressed in their Sunday best. Five ponies graze in the meadow on the right which is now covered with sheltered retirement bungalows. The small brick building on the right was the Phoenix Coal Company's office with the railway station further to the right.

Bottom left: Another gathering in Smallbrook Road as Barnwell's staff and families prepare to board their chara-bancs for their annual summer outing. This was probably on a Sunday as Barnwells would have wanted to keep their grocery shop in the Market Place open throughout the week. The small bus on the left is a solid-wheeled Fiat, AD5053. The driver can have had little light to help illuminate the road from this pair of acetylene lamps.

In September 1903 the *Ross Gazette* reported that the Ross Golf Club was opened on Tuesday 22nd on an excellent site at Alton Court Estate by permission of Mr. G.L. Blake. On this picturesque site on the slope of Penyard Hill a nine-hole course was laid out 'to provide healthy enjoyment and recreation'. On 18 December 1903 their resident professional, J.G. Wingate beat his brother F. Wingate (a professional at Harbourne Golf Club) in a demonstration 18 hole match. By 1906 club members were enjoying matches with Leominster among others, and a summer course with three extra holes was opened on the second field to avoid some of the disruption caused by the military exercises. The club also leased part of their newly-built clubhouse to visiting Army regiments for use as an Officers' Mess. Sharing facilities with units in training was not popular and the club's early years were difficult and membership was low. In 1911 the club had 83 members; its income was £438 13s. 4d. with a surplus of £6 13s. By 1912 numbers had risen to 104 and a professional named Croyden had been employed. Weekly and monthly competitions were organised for gentlemen and lady members. S.H. Deakin of Weir End became their energetic president continually extolling 'The picturesque and sporting course, attractive to visitors of the leisured classes who invariably play golf, which is an asset to the town'. Unfortunately few of the town's photographers bothered to take any photographs of this minority sport which has now become so popular.

King George V's coronation on 22 June 1911 was marked by festivities across the country and a day off school for the children. In the morning rain, soldiers of the South Wales Borderers Regiment head the procession towards the parish church accompanied by the usual group of small boys. The canopy of Gardner's grocery shop sheltered some towns-folk without umbrellas. Part of the message on this card, sent four days later reads:

The festivities here were great and passed expectations in the decorations and illuminations part of it. I joined in the procession to the church in the morning as a member of the Druids. You can see part of the procession in this postcard so you can gather by it that it fell little short of the grand affair in London. The weather was stormy ... but in the evening there was an open air concert in the Prospect. Saturday the cricket match was against Ledbury & we got well beaten. I made 11 runs and was then caught at the wicket. Starting evening work at the Bank now. Much love Bertie.'

Right top: In 1912 the *Daily Mail* organized a series of Aerial Tours of Britain. Expectations in Ross were high and hundreds paid to enter the golf course where Henri Salmet was expected to land on 19 July. Salmet piloted a 50hp Bleriot monoplane and was the chief flying instructor at the Bleriot School for pilots at Hendon Airfield in Middlesex. He was a friend of Louis Bleriot, the pioneer aviation engineer who, in 1909, was the first pilot to cross the English Channel. A small fault and bad weather delayed Salmet at Raglan on the 19th and the townspeople walked disconsolately home. His engine was repaired by the next day when he flew to Ross and became the second airman to land an aeroplane in Herefordshire. He is seen here alighting to the applause of the townspeople and the soldiers of the Sherwood Foresters who marshalled the crowds. Surprisingly this postcard is autographed by 'de Havilland', a young man destined to become an important name in British aviation, but acting then as ground crew for the tour. In the background of this Beeston photograph is the golf club-house.

Centre: The motor car might have made its appearance in Ross in 1900, but for many it was a novelty that would never replace horse power, This did not change for many until the widespread use of motor power in all sorts of different applications during the 1914–18 war proved the internal combustion engine was here to stay. Well turned out horses and carriages attracted attention just as much in Edwardian times as they do at shows today. These two immaculate turn-outs await the judges at a long forgotten show, which Colman Debenham photographed for posterity about 1910.

Left: The *Ross Gazette* of 26 January 1911 carried a graphic report on organised badger digging, quite alien to our modern concepts of sport. Capt. P.B. Huth, who had established a badger digging club in Kent and Sussex, visited the Ross area with his pack of terriers. For the next fortnight he enjoyed his so-called 'sport' with plenty of local people to help. Backed up with plentiful supplies of beer, cider and beef sandwiches for his teams of diggers he killed 12 badgers. His exploits left an ugly legacy demonstrated on this particularly gruesome photograph of five badgers dug out of their winter slumber and killed. At least it does not appear that they were subjected to baiting with dogs, but were killed on capture.

Peace celebrations attracted crowds to the procession in Gloucester Road in November 1918. At last the grim days of the war were over and the relief is evident on everyone's face, although for many families much loved menfolk would never return to Ross.

Top: The Ross Carnival Committee in 1926. Back row from left to right: H. Longford, W.B. Coates, T. Bulman, J. Pearson, Maj. Curling, Col. MacMillan, A. Bird, F. Foxwell and T. Dazeley. Front row: G. Cater, G. Arrowsmith, B.G. Abel, Miss Rawlings, J. Brown, Mrs. E. Hart, Mrs. Abel, L. Ayres.

Bottom left: These pretty sisters all deserve a prize in the fancy dress parade.

Bottom right: Butcher Webb with his splendidly decorated bicycle.

Sombre top-hatted councillors, dignitaries and townspeople process quietly to St. Mary's to mourn the passing of their well-loved King Edward VII on 6 May 1910 after a reign of only 10 years.

Resplendent in his new bandmaster's uniform, John Preedy of Liskeard Cottages, Station Street, prepares for another parade at the head of Ross Town Band. As Band secretary in 1928 he had just helped raise funds to equip the whole band with new uniforms. They had cost £110 12s. 1d., less 12% discount! The money was raised by an appeal fund backed by Ross Urban District Council.

Ross Town Band march along Gloucester Road at the head of a carnival. Preceding them, a policeman escorts a 'convict' with his truncheon drawn in case of possible trouble, under the watchful eye of his superintendent. The band's policy of starting to train boys and young men so there was a developing group to add to the nucleus of competent musicians is clear from this photograph. The boy in short trousers and the young men without uniforms show this policy working. Note the ladies fashions — cloche hats and knee-length dresses help to date this photograph to 1925–30.

Ross Town Band started life as the band of the local Volunteers who, in April 1908, were reformed into the Territorial Army. This was partly due to organisational shortcomings which had been demonstrated in the Boer War, which had led Lord Haldane, Secretary of State for War, to enact a series of reforms under the 1907 Territorial and Reserve Forces Act. The new Company commander saw no need for the old band so the members resigned as a body, keeping their instruments for some of them belonged to the town who had originally raised the funds to purchase them. Some of the men worked for Perkins and Bellamy's foundry who encouraged them to start a short-lived work's band which soon became the Ross Town Band. They raised money for local charities, especially the Cottage Hospital, by playing at major events in the town and at evening concerts at Crossville and the Prospect, and took part in competitions as far away as London.

Despite the passage of time, a sense of Ross' community spirit comes through to us nowadays when looking at these old photographs. In pre-Welfare State days such fund-raising events were vital to everyone as it was essential to support local clubs and charity organisations for there was nothing else to fall back on in times of need. Illness, unemployment and even old age could lead to the workhouse which everyone avoided if at all possible. Events and celebrations were reported in detail in the *Ross Gazette* for townspeople to read and enjoy again their shared memories. Very seldom were photographs used to illustrate these reports. Postcards of the events were usually on sale the day after when it was so fresh in peoples' minds that captions were unnecessary.

CHAPTER NINE

Elections

Local elections seldom raised much interest among the electorate, but the March 1907 Herefordshire County Council elections provided an unexpected contest in Ross when Stephen Deakin of Weir End opposed Henry Southall who had been a councillor for 12 years. In the event Deakin lost, having 383 votes to Southall's 385.

Captain Percy Arthur Clive, M.P. volunteered for service with his regiment, the Grenadier Guards, in the Boer War of 1899–1902. He returned unscathed to continue his Parliamentary career in Westminster and in 1908 successfully contested a by-election in the South Herefordshire constituency for the Unionists, winning by 1,019 votes. He had a London house in Chester Street but lived most of the year at Whitfield, a red brick and stone mansion at Wormbridge where he was chief landowner and lord of the manor. As a Herefordshire man it was felt that he understood local feelings and certainly enjoyed considerable support from his family and friends. An energetic and able young man, he quickly became Assistant Private Secretary to the Chancellor of the Exchequer. With his wife's active support his vigorous campaign in the 1910 election led him again to success. On the outbreak of the First World War he rejoined his regiment in the trenches of Flanders where he fought with distinction. He was wounded twice and was killed in 1917 at the age of 45 trying to rescue a wounded colleague.

Stephen Deakin setting off for a meeting during the 1907 County Council elections from his committee rooms in Heins musical instrument shop at 5 Gloucester Road, still recognisable today as the Wine Rack. The placard reads: 'VOTE FOR DEAKIN. A man of Business Ability. Up to date Ideas. Undoubted Energy. Staunch Supporter of all Local and County Institutions.'

Tilley & Sons of Ledbury printed thousands of these postcards of Capt. and Mrs. Clive to publicise his election meetings around the constituency. The reverse of the one illustrated announced a public meeting in the schoolroom at St. Weonards.

Although at that time only 60% of men were enfranchised, this in no way dimmed people's political enthusiasm and crowds of Clive's supporters blocked Cantilupe Road and celebrated with him on his arrival in Ross after his victory. Clive is wearing a fur-collared coat and is standing in a car hidden by the jubilant crowd who attached ropes and pulled it around the town. Alfred Ursell's yard full of sculptures, monuments and gravestones creates a bizarre, almost surreal background to the festivities. A few days later, when the fuss had died down, he presented his ablest helpers with handsome certificates. The Edwardians very apparent enthusiasm for politics was quite different to the modern attitudes of indifference and scepticism.

CHAPTER TEN

The Military in Ross

The commencement of the Boer War in 1899 produced an outbreak of patriotic fervour unseen before in England, especially as the Boers won considerable initial success. In Ross, this enthusiasm was translated into a practical application by raising two drafts of volunteers for the war effort; one in 1900 and the second in 1901, to help conquer the upstart Boer republics of the Orange Free State and Transvaal. These republics of Dutch origin really only wanted to be left to run their own affairs and mine the rich veins of gold and diamonds found there. They enjoyed considerable world-wide support in their struggle against the might of the British Empire. On Tuesday 16 January 1900, 22 men from B Company, 1st Herefordshire Rifle Volunteer Corps left Ross for training with the Kings Shropshire Light Infantry. They formed a Service Company for supply work, essential but unglamorous labour without which no army can win a campaign.

The victory over the Boers saw the British Empire at the zenith of its power. King Edward VII's coronation almost coincided with the end of the war and was a moment for the country to proclaim its patriotism and loyalty to a popular monarch. Flags of all sorts decorated the Market House as local dignitaries made solemn speeches from the steps surrounded by a phalanx of soldiers, firemen, police and cheerful townspeople.

PEACE. PEACE. PEACE.

The INHABITANTS of ROSS and
DISTRICT are invited to MEET
at the MARKET HALL

At 7.30

THIS (MONDAY) EVENING,

TO SING

"GOD SAVE THE KING."

HENRY M. PURCHAS,
Chairman of the Urban District Council.

ERNEST R. DAVIES,
Clerk,

Council's Offices, Ross,
2nd June, 1902.

Stratford and Trotter, Printers, "Gazette" Office, Ross.

Above: The whole town was expected to congregate in the centre of Ross to celebrate the peace in 1902.

Right: The Hildersley campsite viewed from the water-works on Chase Hill in 1906, when a visiting officer described it as 'An ideal campsite protected from bleak winds by adjacent hills, well drained and very convenient to the town'.

RETURN OF THE VOLUNTEERS.

With martial airs, and ringing cheers,
Ross welcomes home her Volunteers.
The signal's down! in runs the train;
Tommy and Topsy meet again.
Gone are the horrors of the veldt,
And now a different pang is felt;
And faces that he long had missed,
Exchange fond glances, and are kissed.
"Fall in!" the burly Captain cries;
"Attention!" fixes wandering eyes;
"Form fours!" then comes the rum, tum, tum;
The blatant brass, and rolling drum.
Cheers rend the heavens from surging crowd;
But homeward Tommy's not allowed.
With faces bronzed by Afric's sun,
They march to music, see the fun.
The old familiar streets are trod,
Each wending to the House of God.
And Tommy treads the "sacred aisle,"
And sits him down in pews awhile.
Perchance the pew where mother sat,
When Tommy's name was given and that.
The hymns are sung, the prayers are said,
And bowed in prayer each sinner's head.
"Praise God from Whom all blessings flow."
The signal's given, and all now go
To see the Mayor bare his head,
And move his lips while "welcome's" said;
To Tommy hand the enveloped deed,
And invite him to a sumptuous feed.
The cheers go up, the echoes ring!
En masse all sing, "God save the King."

A. J. B.

Ross, June 7th, 1902.

Above: 'Return of the Volunteers' from the local newspaper in June 1902.

Rght: The Staffordshire Regiment at camp and on parade at Hildersley, the Alton Lane campsite. The lighter round marks on their parade ground show the sites of bell tents of previous regiments' camps. The houses in Camp Road are easily recognisable and the background trees, shown on contemporary maps as orchards, have since been replaced by houses as Ross has expanded to its present population of nearly 10,000.

Between £15 and £20 was needed to equip each man, and with only £9 being provided by the government, the remainder had to be found either by the men themselves or by their regiment. The first draft of 22 volunteers enjoyed a short furlough (leave) after training and were treated to a dinner at the King's Head at their officers' expense before they left with the K.S.L.I. from the Royal Albert Dock, London aboard the *Minerva* on 1 March.

There was a local collection in Ross for 'a comfort fund' to provide extra clothing like woollen socks and Balaclava helmets, and for their commanding officer to buy extras like chocolate, cigarettes and beer to make their life easier when they were thousands of miles from home. During 1900–02 many letters of support appeared in the *Ross Gazette*, which was also full of reports from the war zone. Prayers for their safe return were offered every week at St. Mary's and other churches. As a support company they performed the tough, monotonous, essential work of keeping the front line troops supplied and only came under fire once, on 17 May 1900 at Winberg. Privates E.H. Adams and J.P. Smith died of enteric fever during the campaign.

A second contingent left Ross in June 1901 as the fortunes of war swung in Britain's favour. After a period of guerrilla warfare, peace was eventually signed on 1 June 1902. The citizens of Ross went 'peace making' around the Market House and 'did their duty celebrating peace as loyal and patriotic Englishmen', when these handbills were distributed (opposite). The volunteers returned to Ross on 5 June to a heroes' welcome and a celebratory dinner at the King's Head. A year later a memorial service was held at St. Mary's for their fallen comrades, for many Herefordshire men had served in various regiments throughout the war, 44 losing their lives in this last major colonial war. For its size Ross volunteered proportionally more men than any other town in the United Kingdom.

Top: Resplendent in their best walking-out uniforms, this regiment is apparently on church parade as it marches off the campsite towards St. Mary's Church.

Bottom: To everyone's great delight a soldier in the obstacle race gets a good soaking on the regimental sports day, amusing a small audience of squaddies and the elegantly dressed civilians watching. More buckets of water are readied for the next batch of unfortunate victims who took the soaking with good humour.

The eye-catching sign on the gable-end of the George Hotel overlooks a traffic-free Gloucester Road as the 3rd battalion of the Welsh Regiment marches back to camp. Led by its goat mascot and regimental band it provided a fine martial sight. Escorting them along the road the little boys of Ross imagine themselves as soldiers, not realising the horrors the impending 1914–1918 war would bring to them all. The old shops and houses on the south side of Gloucester Road were demolished with the George in 1960 and a row of new shops built.

Over the years many different regiments enjoyed the varied delights of the Volunteers campsite at Hildersley, one of 11 such camps scattered across the country. Battalions of the Yorkshire, Lancashire, Derbyshire, Staffordshire, Sherwood Foresters, Welsh, Shropshire, Gloucestershire, Worcestershire, and Herefordshire Regiments and probably many others camped there for their annual training. Many returned year after year although the Welsh used sites in Wales three years out of four. Between 200 and 1,000 soldiers would spend two or three weeks in camp before being replaced by another regiment. Such large numbers of men benefited the local economy very considerably and Ross went to some expense to encourage the use of the camp. One year, for example, local subscriptions raised £40 to hire an extra drill ground at Weir End and the street lights were left alight till midnight. It was worth the extra expense as a fortnight's camp was worth about £10,000 to local shopkeepers and suppliers. On one occasion 18 special trains ran into Ross station and a temporary siding on the campsite in one day, bringing 900 men and their horses from the Royal Gloucestershire Hussars, the Queen's Own Worcestershire Hussars and the Shropshire Yeomanry for a three-week training exercise! There were inevitable occasional accidents, and three horses had to be put down during the camp.

To feed these fit young soldiers, busy on manoeuvres in the countryside, at drill on the grass parade ground and at target practice on the adjoining rifle range, was a major logistical undertaking. C. Preece

Casualties on an unprecedented scale soon brought home the horrors of warfare to the people of England in 1914 and civilian volunteers quickly organised themselves to do something to help their menfolk abroad. Henry Palmer photographed a dozen volunteer nurses in Ross preparing medical dressings for use in field hospitals in France, Italy, the Middle East and the Balkans. Ladies were able to join all branches of the services to free more men for active duty. Their efforts in munitions factories and all sorts of other war work were eventually rewarded in 1918 with the right to vote.

of Hereford was contracted to supply 1,500lbs. of meat daily, whilst Little of Ross supplied 500 quarters of bread (1,000 loaves). T. Pitt of Holt near Worcester sent 8,000 new laid eggs and B. Murdoch of Hope Mansell 80 gallons of milk. Bussell & Pike supplied potatoes and Llewellyn & Son 40 tons of coal. Alton Court Brewery had the beer and mineral water concession. Bussell & Pike also supplied forage for the horses including 600 quarters of oats, 100 tons of hay and 60 tons of moss litter for bedding.

These military camps also provided a lively social scene and were long remembered for dances organised by the officers and sergeants, well attended concerts in the marquees, camp fire sing-songs and military tattoos. There were Sunday church parades and military concerts at the camp and in the town. In addition there were football and cricket matches against local and other military teams. Regimental sports days could attract an audience of over 200 spectators as soldiers competed on the assault course, at tent pegging and horse racing. Some of the local ladies raised funds during the year for a Mission Room where off duty soldiers could read, write home or take part in a religious service. Everyone seemed to enjoy these training camps which finished at the end of the First World War when social conditions were very different.

'The men under canvas behaved splendidly and were a credit to their regiments', the Mayor was reported to say at the end of one camp. Surprisingly there were hardly any cases of drunkenness or

These Women's Land Army girls seem ready for any job they were given to do on the land. Dressed in stout boots, breeches, leather gaiters, overalls and hats they are equipped to drive horses, milk cows, make hay, hoe weeds, dig, cut bean poles and even keep rabbits. Their instructress at Howle Farm, Walford (where it is believed this photograph was taken) must have been well pleased with her recruits.

disorderly behaviour in the town. Most of the men regarded the events as a sort of paid holiday in the countryside and looked forward to them eagerly as 'a bit of a laugh'.

The campsite saw many changes in use from its pasture land of 1873, when the Ross and Monmouth railway divided the lower fields of Alton Court farm in two parts. Ross Golf Club started life here on a nine hole course laid out on both sides of the railway track in 1903. Three years later the Club published the following advertisement in the *Ross Gazette*: 'Ross Golf Links. Trespassers picking mushrooms will be prosecuted. 15 August 1906. T.H. Combes. Secretary'. From 1903 the Club shared the greens and fields and their club house with visiting army regiments on summer training camps. The Golf Club moved to Rudhall in 1925 leaving the site very little used in the inter-war years. The Town Council briefly considered the premises for an Isolation Hospital but even at £100 they were found to be too old and unsuitable.

The site quickly resumed its role of training camp at the outbreak of war in 1939. In the later years of the war it became a Prisoner of War camp. In 1946 there were proposals to turn these huts at the Drill Hall Camp into accommodation for squatters, and despite the conditions some desperate people lived there until they were rehoused. Alton Lane was widened and reconstructed and in the 1960s light industrial units were built along it giving much needed employment to the whole of the Ross on Wye area.

Ross on Wye saw an influx of soldiers and evacuees at the beginning of the Second World War, and the Army camp at Hildersley saw many regiments pass through on training exercises. At the height of the Battle of Britain on 12 September 1940 the men of the 9th Battalion, Royal Sussex Regiment march smartly along Gloucester Road past a dais where the Lord Lieutenant of Herefordshire, Lord Somers of Eastnor, took the salute. A quiet crowd of townspeople look on. As a wartime precaution to confuse the enemy in case of invasion 'Herefordshire' has been painted out on the fascia board of South Herefordshire Agricultural Co-operative Society's shop. Signposts on the roads were removed for the same reason, leading to huge confusion for lorry drivers everywhere.

CHAPTER ELEVEN

Wilton

Although locally Wilton is regarded as part of Ross on Wye, it is in fact part of the parish of Bridstow. In Old English Wilton means 'farm among the willows' — osier beds for cutting withies for basket-making survived here until the last century with basket-making works at the Hope and Anchor Inn just upstream.

The river Wye is shallow here and the ford has been in use since time immemorial. It is safe to assume that boats were used when the water was too deep to ford and these developed into a regular ferry service. After 40 people lost their lives when an overloaded ferry was overwhelmed in a flood, a toll bridge was built in 1599. Over the years it was repaired regularly and widened twice and, like Hereford's bridge, it lost an arch during the Civil War.

As an essential war time measure it was widened in 1939 to cope with the anticipated increase in traffic. The sundial that stood in one of the central recesses on the east side of the bridge, was moved to the west side during the 1992 widening scheme. Erected in 1712 by Jonathan Barrow of Bridstow it bears the following verse, now very weathered:

> Esteem thy precious time
> Which pass so swift away
> Prepare then for eternity
> And do not make delay.

On the north side of Wilton Bridge lies Wilton Castle, built in 1141. It is unusually situated, being close to the river on low-lying ground. Many border castles were built on high ground to dominate their surroundings by their presence, but Wilton was built shortly after the Norman conquest to defend the ford and later guarded the bridge over the Wye. The owner's endeavours to remain neutral in the Civil War provoked the Royalists into burning the castle one Sunday whilst the family was at church. A Victorian house was built amid the ruins and as this is being written the old castle is being extensively renovated.

In the last 200 years Wilton slowly developed by the wharves along the river bank and along the road to the bridge out of reach of the winter floods. Inns and hotels for tourists appeared. In the 1960s the orchards between the Wye and the new A40 road were replaced by houses. The old bridge still makes an attractive entrance to Ross on Wye from Hereford and the west.

Above: William Call started his photographic career in Chepstow, later moving to the 'County Studio' in Monmouth. He specialised in architectural photography but also published many excellent local views such as this one of a donkey cart crossing Wilton Bridge on its way to Ross market.

Left: The sundial on the bridge was erected in 1712 by Jonathon Barrow of Bridstow.

A 1930s view of Wilton bridge from the west showing the shallows in the centre where the original ford was situated. A tower of Wilton Castle apparently rises from a bridge pillar. In previous centuries trees were not allowed to grow along the river banks as they would obstruct the tow ropes on laden barges. Now that only a few boats use the river, quite large willow thickets have appeared, preventing access from the old towpaths.

Top: The present house at Wilton Castle was built in the 19th century inside the remains of the old castle, which provide a picturesque background for Mrs. Walsh's gardens.

Bottom: 'Taken in September 1907 at Wilton Castle' is the pencilled note on the reverse of this postcard. If only everyone had taken the trouble to note 'who, where and when' on the backs of photographs researchers' lives would be made much easier! This photograph portrays Captain Lewis Paxton Walsh J.P. and Mrs. Walsh preparing for a drive in their landau with William Ford in the driving seat. (I am indebted to Fred Druce for the names of this group)

"Wilton Court" Ross-on-Wye

▼ ▼ ▼

Beautiful XVIth Century Old World House and Lawns on Banks of the River Wye

Dining Room Separate Tables	Fully Sprung Interior Mattresses	Own Garden Produce
Central Heating	Hot & Cold in all Bedrooms	

Under personal supervision of Resident Proprietors : Mr. and Mrs. F. G. OAKLEY

Telegrams and Phone : Ross-on-Wye 2569

A.A.   Stamp for Brochure   R.A.C.

✳ ✳ Ross-on-Wye & District Hoteliers' & Caterers' Association Member

Top: To the west of Wilton was the Boat House Café, idyllically placed on the banks of the River Wye. Bypassed now by the A40 dual carriageway, it has become a private house.

Left: This advertisement for Wilton Court appeared in a 1950s Ross on Wye guidebook in a bid to welcome the increasing numbers of tourists exploring the beauties of the area. Things that are now expected, such as separate tables in the dining room and interior sprung mattresses, were worthy of inclusion in the advertisement

1960s postcards can show just as dramatic changes as their Edwardian predecessors. For a period in the 1950s and '60s Bennett's, who owned Wilton Garage beside the new dual carriageway roundabout, also ran a large caravan park in the orchard next to their premises. Their garage has now been replaced with a modern shop and a busy forecourt with fuel pumps to supply all the needs of the traffic using this junction. Orchard Caravan Park has lost its caravans and is now unrecognisable with its rows of houses along Orchard Way.

The shallows just below Wilton Bridge provided a fordable crossing point until the bridge was built in 1599. These shallows stretch further downstream and gave the local Boy Scouts somewhere to cool off after parade, far away from any scandalised prying eyes. Only 15 of the 67 appear to be wearing bathing costumes as they pose for Dickie Davies's camera, their clothes piled on the shingle in this delightfully innocent photograph. Baden-Powell's Boy Scout movement was popular as it was non-denominational and appealed to boys of all classes. Six older men, one holding a rope, watch in case anyone gets into difficulties. The Wye appears deceptively safe but the newspapers reported an average of one drowning a year. People bathing in the river also ran the risk of disease from the town's untreated sewage. It was only after years of pressure from townspeople that a swimming pool was built in 1973 and apart from an occasional photograph like this, such scenes became part of local folk memory. The white house in the centre is Wilton Grange and the brick one on the right is Wilton Hall. These shallows are now unapproachable due to the rapid growth of trees and bushes on the river bank.

APPENDIX

Victorian and Edwardian Photographers in Ross

The following is based on a list compiled by Michael Hallet. I have added more information from archive material, advertisements and original photographs for more personal and business details and extended dates.

Alfred George Beeston was in business for 18 years from 1899 to 1917, first at 2 Broad Street then at 21 Broad Street. He sold his business at no. 21 to Henry Palmer on 1 March 1917.

Richard Britten Bustin established the first photographers' studio in the county in Hereford in 1856. With his family's support he ran his photographers' business in Gloucester Road, Ross, from 1870 to 1900.

Mrs. M. Bustin & Son, Hereford and Ross, 1872 to 1879.

Mr. and Mrs. Bustin and Son, Hereford and Ross, 1891 to 1900.

Messrs. Bustin, Ross on Wye 1898. On 19 April 1900 a photographic studio at 14 Gloucester Road was advertised for sale in the *Ross Gazette*. This was almost certainly Bustin's studio and was later used by R.E. Davies.

William T. Casson advertised as a photographer and coach builder in Gloucester Road in 1900.

Jno. Cropper had a photographic business in Broad Street in 1859.

B. Davies was mentioned in the *Ross Gazette* in July 1900 as a photographer.

Richard Edwin Davies (Dickie) had a studio in Cantilupe Road from 1905 to 1909. From 1910 until the 1950s he operated from the Wye Studio, 14 Gloucester Road, advertising about 1950 as a photographic dealer opposite the Post Office. In 1937 his home address was 'The Shrubbery', Camp Road.

Colman Debenhan had a studio in Gloucester Road, opposite the Post Office, from 1909 to 1916. He sold his business in 1916 when conscripted into the army. He specialised in children and wedding photography and sold photographic materials according to his 1910 advertisements.

George Henry Finch occupied the Rembrandt Studio, Gloucester Road. 1890–91. He published real photographic postcards in 1910.

Maurice H. Hack of Ross and Cheltenham had a studio in Gloucester Road from 1900 to 1905. In July 1900 he donated photographs at the Wesleyan Sunday School Fete.

Henry Palmer bought Beeston's business at 21 Broad Street on 1 March 1917. In November he installed electricty in a studio opposite the Post Office for indoor photography. He photographed many local families for them to send to servicemen abroad to remind them of loved ones at home.

Mrs. Arthur H. Pearson occupied the Studio, Gloucester Road from 1905 to 1909.

Charles Smith was an early phoographer at Vaga Place, Dock Street between 1863 and 1885.

Alfred William Ursell was a monumental mason and photographer in Cantilupe Road from 1905 to 1909.

William Harding Warner was another early photographer in Gloucester Road from 1862 to 1867.

Herbert Edward Wilkins used the Park Studio, Archenfield Road from 1902 to 1926. He published real photographic postcards from 1908.

George William Young, 1873-1938. His grandfather and father owned a lime quarry and kiln in Howle Hill, Walford. At an early age he learnt photography in Ross. His descendants still have his photographs of Queen Victoria's Diamond Jubilee celebrations at the Market House. He moved to Brecon Road, Abergavenny about 1900 and used a studio at 8 High Street, Abergavenny until 1906. For family reasons he moved back to Belle View, Bull's Hill, Walford in 1907. In 1909 he reopened the old lime kilns, and when his sister married he took over from her as sub-postmaster at Howle Hill Post Office in 1910. He built the 'Floral Studio' next door to the Post Office where he lived until 1917. Photographing aeroplanes and pilots at Farnborough and other places during the war made him a lot of money. About 1920 he moved to Clytha House, 44 New Street in Ross and had a photographic studio from 1926 in Cantilupe Road in the premises now occupied by S. and R. Taxis. He published postcards of the area and the local Council commissioned him to take photographs of the slum clearances. He was also a very competant artist and cartoonist.

George William Young

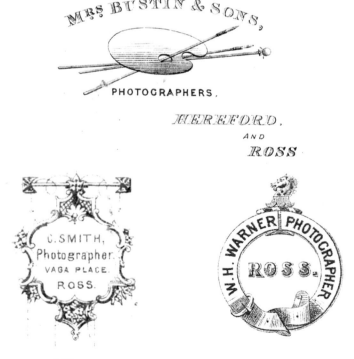

Index

Also from Logaston Press

Knights Templar and Knights Hospitaller in Herefordshire
by Audrey Tapper   ISBN 1 904396 35 6   £4.95

If these two Orders of knights and the county of Herefordshire are mentioned in the same breath, then surely Garway and Dinmore might follow in the next as they were the main Templar and Hospitaller houses in the county. Garway certainly has the most substantial Templar remains in the church tower, the 'saracenic' chancel arch within the church, the remains of the round nave outside and the old columbarium in the adjacent farm buildings. Dinmore eventually became totally responsible for the properties of both Orders in the counties of Herefordshire and Shropshire when the Templar possessions passed to the Hospitallers early in the 14th century. Yet Callow, Harewood, Hereford (in connection with both Orders), Rowlestone, Sutton St. Michael, Upleadon, Welsh Newton and Wormbridge all played their part in supporting the knights and might not come to mind at all.

How did the Orders obtain these properties? What was their function and how were they managed? How were they used to promote the work of the Orders in England and in the Holy Land? What happened to the properties of the Templars when the Order was disbanded in the early 1300s? This booklet answers these and other questions, providing a brief history of the knights and delving into the grants of land and property in the county.

Herefordshire Folklore
by Roy Palmer   ISBN 1 873827 58 X   £12.95

Roy Palmer presents the folklore of the county as a series of themes that embrace landscape, buildings, beliefs, work, seasons and people. In so doing, ten chapters are crafted that can stand alone or be read as a whole, each full of snippets of insight into the county's past in a way that adds to anyone's enjoyment of Herefordshire. Having read the book, features of the landscape, for example, will appear as landmarks associated with certain folk beliefs adding to their interest and to one's own sense of 'belonging' to the county.

Much, but by no means all, of the information presented here first appeared in Roy Palmer's *Folklore of Hereford and Worcester*, published by Logaston Press in 1992, when Herefordshire was joined with Worcestershire. Additional research has revealed more remedies that have been handed down within families; the occasional old ballad or song sheet hidden behind wallpaper or in the bottom of trunks; further snippets of oral knowledge—and new 'customs' that have been revived or even created.

Also from Logaston Press

Herefordshire Past & Present—An Aerial View
by Ruth E. Richardson & Chris Musson   ISBN 1 904396 20 8   £14.95

The focus of this book is partly on features that make Herefordshire distinct, and partly on those which are barely visible, or not visible at all, on the ground. The aim is thus to show not just some wonderful Herefordshire scenery and landmarks, but also how aerial photography and the techniques which it uses continues to develop our appreciation and knowledge of the county. In these photographs it is possible to see evidence of a Bronze Age circle, of Iron Age farms and settlements, of medieval mills and settlements. The book also allows one to appreciate the line of transport networks, from the Roman crossing of the Wye near Kenchester, through tramroads, canals and railways to modern bypasses. Thumbnail sketches help explain pictures of cropmarks at *Magnis*, rabbit warren farming at Willey, the Grandmontine Priory at Craswall, the multiple bailey system at Kingsland Castle and the development of Longtown. There are also startling photos of the major towns which are such a distinctive feature of the county.

Full colour

Tales from Herefordshire Graves and Burials
by Nicola Goodwin   ISBN 1 904396 44 5   £9.95

This book glimpses the lives of some of those buried in Herefordshire, from the obscure graves of young children, some of them unbaptised, through to those of well heeled knights, bishops and earls.

Quite a mixture of people have ended their days in Herefordshire's soil—a Russian princess, a Hungarian general, a little known King of England, one of the successful British commanders in the War of American Independence, a few saints, and possibly Hamlet, Prince of Denmark as well as Amr, the son of King Arthur.

A few explorers also emanated from Herefordshire and returned to the county to die, or are commemorated in churches, among them Robert Masters who sailed with Cavendish on the second English circumnavigation of the Globe; and Richard Jordan who accompanied Richard Lander in his exploration of the River Niger.

There are two survivors from the Battle of Waterloo and one from Rorke's Drift. There is the godfather of Horatio Nelson, a murdered vicar, and a midwife who successfully saw to 526 births. Tablets record deaths from a wolf and by jumping from a moving stagecoach. There is a tale of Resurrectionists, of a 12th man on a cricket pitch, of someone who had their grave marked by a huge boulder which had to be dragged into the churchyard, knocking down the surrounding wall in the process. The subject of the book may appear morbid, but the tales are usually anything but.